David F

C000199632

PLAYS ONE

David Farr is a writer and director. His plays *The Danny Crowe Show*, *Elton John's Glasses* and *Night of the Soul* have all been published by Faber. As Joint Artistic Director of Bristol Old Vic (2003–5) he has directed *Paradise Lost* by John Milton and Shakespeare's *A Midsummer Night's Dream*, *The Comedy of Errors*, and *Twelfth Night*. He has directed *Coriolanus* and *Julius Caesar* for the RSC, and was Artistic Director of London's Gate Theatre from 1995 to 1998. He becomes Artistic Director of the Lyric Theatre, Hammersmith, in June 2005. His play *The UN Inspector* will open at the National Theatre in June 2005 and is to be published by Faber.

by the same author

ELTON JOHN'S GLASSES
THE NATIVITY
THE DANNY CROWE SHOW
NIGHT OF THE SOUL

DAVID FARR

Plays One

The Odyssey

Crime and Punishment in Dalston

The Nativity

Great Expectations

Introduced by
the author

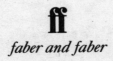

faber and faber

This collection first published in 2005
by Faber and Faber Limited
3 Queen Square, London WC1N 3AU

Typeset by Country Setting, Kingsdown, Kent CT14 8ES
Printed in England by Mackays of Chatham plc, Chatham, Kent

2 4 6 8 10 9 7 5 3 1

Contents

Introduction

These four plays have in common the fact that I wrote none of them. Or, more truthfully, they are all reworkings of existing stories, from the ancient world of Homer to the beginnings of modernism. I have become increasingly interested in addressing the turbulence of our world through looking at archetypal stories in a new way.

The Dickens is the most straightforward adaptation, albeit with a modernist, Freudian slant. The others are more radical. Dostoevsky in Dalston, Homer in an immigration centre, the Nativity with Old Testament stories, the devil and a mad shepherd.

All the plays are intended to be performed with a cast of eight or less. My intention has been to tell big theatrical stories but in a financially manageable way.

I would like to thank all the artists, actors and theatres that helped me develop these plays, in particular Simon Reade, Mehmet Ergen and everyone at the miraculous Arcola Theatre, Harry Ross, Tiffany Watt-Smith, Emma Rice, Caroline Maude, Nancy Meckler, Dave Fishley, everyone at Bristol Old Vic, and Anne Siddons.

THE ODYSSEY

a new retelling
after Homer

for Annie after ten years

The Odyssey in this adaptation was first perfomed on 19 February 2005 at Bristol Old Vic. The cast was as follows:

Odysseus Robert Bowman
Interrogator 1/Thoas/Eurylochos Colin Mace
Athena/Elpinor Dave Fishley
Circe/Mother Mia Soteriou
Maira/Penelope Agni Tsangaridou
Interrogator 2/Dolon Stuart McLoughlin
Musician Stu Barker/Pete

All other parts were played by the company

Director David Farr
Designer Angela Davies
Lighting Chris Davey
Music Stu Barker
Choreography Ann M. Yee
Puppetry Mervyn Millar
Sound Jason Barnes
Fights Terry King
Assistant Director Anne Tipton

Characters

Odysseus
Athena
Interrogator 1 (Roger)
Interrogator 2 (Harold)
Elpinor
Thoas
Dolon
Cyclops
Trojan Man
Trojan Woman
Maira
Aeolus
Circe
Eurylochos
Circe's Maidservants
Tiresias
Odysseus' Mother
Penelope
Old Man (Eumaeus)
Antinoos
Leodes
Puppet Maira
Puppet Abas
Puppet Samira

Greek Sailors / Soldiers
Sheep
Pigs
Cattle of the Sun
Trojans

Act One

PROLOGUE

A man lies washed up and unconscious on the shore of a foreign land. The goddess Athena watches over him.

Athena Don't wake him. The sea's given him a beating. Let him rest.

It's all the sea god's doing. We wanted him released. The nymph Calypso had kept him prisoner for seven years on her island. She made love to him all night and he cried for his wife all day. It was punishment enough. Time to send him home.

Poseidon had other ideas. He sees our hero floating across the ocean on a small raft. The angry god grabs sky and sea and knocks them together like two heads. The winds roar, and on the raft the man's knees tremble.

What comes now to torment me?

What now, cruel gods?

A lonely death on a vast anger?

A wave tears down on him, the raft smashed, the oars ripped from his hands, the mast snapped like a twig, and he's swept under. He grabs for a plank, holds on for dear life as Poseidon hurls wave after wave on top of him. The sea god sees him lose grip of the plank, and leaves him there for dead. Job done.

That's where I come in. Athena the merciful. Always had a soft spot for our general. I send the sea to sleep and batten down the winds – all except the North that drives the half-dead hero to this shore. Through salty eyes he sees the grey land and cries out:

Hear me whoever you are!

I come in need of your solace.

7

I am fugitive from the sea.
I flee the fury of Poseidon.
I am the endless wanderer.
I fall on my knees.
I beg your mercy on my head.

Now he is asleep. Let him snooze on the shores of a strange land. His trials are far from over. If life was just, he would be met by a beautiful maiden, taken to the king's palace and treated as a god, wined and dined, bathed in rich oils, sung songs of his own heroism and given passage home.
But life isn't just, is it?

Athena drifts away. Odysseus awakes and spews water.

Odysseus What country is this?
Violent and savage – without justice?
Or kind, hospitable, gentle to foreigners and of mild demeanour?

Interrogator 1 I'm afraid you'll find it's the former.

Two Interrogators have appeared.

Odysseus Who are you?

Interrogator 1 Stop you right there, mate. We'll be the ones asking the questions. Stand up.

Odysseus tries to rise. Interrogator 1 punches him.

Interrogator 1 I said stand up.

Odysseus I'm trying.

Interrogator 1 Not hard enough.

Odysseus I've just spent three days clinging to wreckage.

Interrogator 1 Spare us the sob stories and stand up.

Odysseus tries to rise. Interrogator 2 punches him and he crumples.

Interrogator 1 Are you deaf or something? I said stand up!

Odysseus How can I stand if you keep . . .

He rises and is punched again. He crumples again.

Interrogator 1 Hmmn. We've got us a tricky one here.

SCENE ONE
THE INTERROGATION

The interrogation room. A table and two chairs. A bare bulb. Odysseus, alone, hears singing. A young woman is singing a song for home. We do not see her.

Woman
This room is not my room.
This bed is not my own.
This pale bulb is not my dawn.
This home is not my home.

These walls are not my walls.
This dream is not my own.
This pale breath is not my breath.
This home is not my home.

These eyes are not my eyes.
This skin is not my skin.
This pale life is not my life.
Till I see my home again.
Till I see my home again.

Odysseus Who is there? Who sings that desperate song for home?

9

Voice We who have lost everything.

Odysseus Who are you?

Voice We are many. The Greeks made sure of that. They razed our city to the ground and scattered us through the world. Now we seek sanctuary but are refused at every port. We are the pariahs of the earth.

Odysseus What was your city?

Voice The greatest city of all. Troy.

Enter the Interrogators with clothes.

Interrogator 1 Put some clothes on. Now then, just a few formalities. I have in my hands a statement of evidence. Do you know what that is?

Odysseus No.

Interrogator 1 No, I didn't think you would. A statement of evidence is a statement that you make in which you give evidence in support of your case. Legally you have ten days in which to submit the form but it's our belief that keeping you in our highly expensive detention centre is a waste of your time and our money when we could be filling this out today and getting you processed. Some people think that interviewing an applicant seconds after they've completed a life-endangering, trauma-inducing journey across half the globe is insensitive, but they're prats. Is that clear?

Interrogator 2 What you saying?

Interrogator 1 I'm just softening him up. (*to Odysseus*) Is that clear?

Odysseus Yes.

Interrogator 1 Good. Now I need to inform you you have a legal right to have a lawyer present but you're not obliged. No, you're right, let's just keep it intimate, shall we? You want tea? Food? No? Good. Anything else I can get you in accordance with the Geneva Convention? Good. How did you get here?

Odysseus I didn't want to come here. A storm . . . washed me up . . .

Interrogator 2 What's he saying?

Interrogator 1 Says he didn't want to come. Says a storm washed him up.

Interrogator 2 A likely story. He's trying to get in under our noses. Bloody illegals.

Odysseus What's he saying?

Interrogator 1 He's casting doubt on your story, mate.

Odysseus Can't he speak my language?

Interrogator 1 No, mate.

Interrogator 2 What's he saying?

Interrogator 1 I'm explaining that you can't understand a word he's saying

Odysseus But you can?

Interrogator 1 Can what?

Interrogator 2 What's he asking?

Interrogator 1 Will you shut up?

Odysseus Speak my language.

Interrogator 1 What?

Odysseus Can you speak my language?

Interrogator 1 Oh yeah. I speak Greek fluent. That's what I'm here for. My language skills. And my diplomacy.

I speak Greek, Babylonian, Minoan, Spartan, Persian, Ethiopian, Mesopotamian – that's a tricky one, I can tell you.

Odysseus What country is this?

Interrogator 1 As if you don't know.

Interrogator 2 What's he saying?

Interrogator 1 He's just being clever.

Interrogator 2 Shall I hit him?

Interrogator 1 Yeah.

Odysseus What did he say?

Interrogator 1 He asked me if he should hit you.

Interrogator 2 hits him.

I said yes. Now, enough of your smart-alec stuff. This form is seventy pages long, I don't want to be here all fucking night. Let's start with an easy one. Why are you here?

Odysseus I told you, I didn't want to come.

Interrogator 1 I'm beginning to lose my patience with you. I could tear this form up right now. And then where would you be? Up shit creek without a visa. Don't you think I know what's really going on? You paid a nice man from whatever godforsaken hole you're from, he guaranteed you access to the promised land, got you a seat on a boat trying to sneak into our waters at night. But the boat was dodgy, at the hint of the first serious wave it capsized and all the poor sods died except you because you've got your advanced swimming proficiency badge. Am I close? Do you realise this happens to the likes of you every fucking night? Another twenty poor sods are washed up dead on our shores with their fake identity cards still tightly gripped in their stone-cold hands. And if you do get here, we're waiting for you to send you back to whatever sewer you come from. So it's a bit of a waste of time isn't it? You're going home, sunshine. You hear me? You're going home.

Interrogator 2 What d'you just say?

Interrogator 1 Gave him the 'You're going home' speech. (*to Odysseus*) You're going home!

Odysseus I want to go home.

Pause.

Interrogator 1 What did you say?

Odysseus I want to go home.

Interrogator 2 What did he say?

Interrogator 1 He's taking the piss.

Interrogator 1 punches Odysseus hard.

Let's get some sense out of you. What's your name? Where are you from? What's your business?

Beat.

Odysseus My name is Odysseus. I am from sun-kissed Ithaca. There stands a tall mountain, leaf-trembling Neritos, with islands dotted round it, close-lying, and mine the last, rough and rugged, but a nurse of great men. I cannot think of a place more beautiful to look at. Twenty years ago I left Ithaca as a general of the Greek army under the great Agamemnon. I commanded the attack on Troy, sacked its sacred citadel. From which I have been driven many ways, on endless journeys, many the cities I have seen, many the minds I have learned of, many the pains I have suffered to my spirit on the wide sea, fighting for my own survival and for the homecoming

13

of my men. My men I could not save, hard though I tried. Their own stubbornness and recklessness condemned them, fools! Eating of the meat of the sun-cattle which was expressly forbidden. Now I alone come to these shores to beg conveyance home to Ithaca, for I have been too long from my people. Nothing is sweeter in the end than wife, parents, country. Nothing is sweeter than home.

Pause.

Interrogator 2 What did he say?

Interrogator 1 Shut it, will ya? (*to Odysseus*) You're insulting my intelligence. I don't like it when people do that. Odysseus is dead. He's been dead ten years – everyone knows that. Now I'm giving you one more chance before I stick you in the mental ward and throw away the key. Who are you?

Odysseus My name is Odysseus. I am from sun-kissed Ithaca. There stands a tall mountain, leaf-trembling Neritos . . .

Interrogator 1 Take him away, Harold.

Odysseus Help me, Athena, daughter of Zeus, give me strength to tell my story.

The two Interrogators stop dead as Odysseus begins his story.

SCENE TWO
THE WANDERINGS OF ODYSSEUS:
THE LOTUS EATERS

Odysseus What we had done to anger the gods I do not know. We victorious Greeks, obliterators of Troy.

Agamemnon sailed home to his own murder. Menelaus to the eternal unhappiness of the marriage bed with the indifferent Helen. But I – unluckiest of all – the gods had worse in store for me. With six strong ships I set sail for home. This was the beginning of ten years.

We are on a boat. Odysseus' ship home.

Odysseus Men. Victorious Greeks. My army! Troy lies decimated at your feet! Never again will that city stand tall against us. Never again will its leaders defy our great justice! Never again will its infidel people presume to challenge our superiority! But now our thoughts turn homeward. The winds are set fair. The ocean is calm. Our ships stand tall and proud. Six days it will take us to reach Ithaca! Your wives will greet you with their welcoming arms. Ten long years have creased their faces, they worry they no longer attract you, but you will find them more beautiful than ever! Your children will rush to see you. You will not recognise them, nor they you. But every day spent with them will replenish your image in their hearts. Oh my friends, the best of this adventure is yet to come. Victory over enemies is sweet but the return from victory the sweetest of all!

Distant thunder.

Sailor Storm approaching, general.

Eerie silence.

Odysseus It's passing by. Don't worry, friends! The gods are our protectors! They will ensure we come to no harm.

A storm shatters the boat.

Sailors Pull in the mainsail!

Ropes are handed out to the audience.

Odysseus/Sailors Hold her tight! Gather her in! Don't let go! Pull! Pull! Keep her upright! (*Etc.*)

The storm ends.

Odysseus Well done, everyone.

The storm begins again.

Grab the oars! Row through it! Row!

The Sailors row.

Sailors
Night springs from heaven.
Ship on the current flies.
Sail shreds into seven.
Wind spits in our eyes.

The boat collapses.

Odysseus Hold tight men. Row! Hold tight!

Men scatter. Only Odysseus maintains the oars to the bitter end.

Nine days later. The men awaken in a strange land.

Elpinor Odysseus? Odysseus!

Odysseus Here, Elpinor.

Elpinor Where are we?

Odysseus Miles from our course. Buffeted for nine days. Two ships lost and all their men. What have we done to anger the gods?

Elpinor Nothing, my general. They smiled on us through ten years of war. They won't desert us now.

Odysseus You have always been loyal to me, Elpinor.

Elpinor You have given me reason.

Odysseus What island is this?

Elpinor The air has a rare fragrance.

Soldier 1 The purple blossom sways on the trees.

Soldier 2 The breeze lulls us like a blanket.

Odysseus I can hear soft music. It makes me want to sleep again. We must focus. I want to get straight home without delay. Gather the men.

Elpinor Men! Your general wishes to address you.

Odysseus The gods that have brought us nothing but bounty now test our resolve. It is right they should do so. They demand that we return from the war as we fought the war, with strength of spirit and quickness of mind. I know we will not be found wanting. I have sent two of my finest officers, Thoas and Dolon, to find out who lives on this island and to bring back food. Once they have returned we will fix our ships and be on our way. Trust me: these two men are dependable to the last and will not forget their duty.

Enter the two men, clad in flowery garlands, peace signs, etc.

Odysseus Thoas? Dolon?

Elpinor What the hell are you playing at?

Thoas Chill out, man. Deal with that anger.

Odysseus Dolon – what happened? I sent you to find food and wine to hasten our voyage home. Who has done this to you?

Dolon (*pitying*) Ugh – would you look at that.

Odysseus Look at what?

Dolon That weight of anxiety on your shoulder. Cast it off, man, it's giving you grief. Let me help you, man.

Elpinor Address your general with respect!

Thoas What greater respect is there than love? Listen up, everyone. These guys on this island, OK, they have got it sorted. They were sitting in a circle when we found them, just smiling and shit, totally chilled, some naked, some not, just hanging out – they took one look at us and our uniforms and one of them just said the whole thing – why war? Why war?

Dolon Blatantly.

Thoas They gave us this flower to eat, man.

Dolon And they were singing this song. Listen to the words, man.

> We are the lotus eaters.
> We are the lotus eaters.
> Yes we are. Yes we are.
> We are the lotus eaters.
> We are the lotus eaters.
> Yes we are. Yes we are.

Thoas Totally.

Odysseus Let's get out of here.

Thoas No no no, my general. No comprende? Major mindshift here, man. Me not going nowhere. Me staying with the lotus army. Dolon's staying too. And we want everyone to stay with us.

Elpinor Men, you are tired. You have been at war for a long time. What we need is to get home.

Thoas What we *need* is some space to think our thoughts. We've won the battle, now let's win the war. Listen to me, everyone. Come with us to the lotus eaters. They've enough for everyone. Look – here's some. Take it. One bite of the flower and all the nightmares can be forgotten. Every man you killed can float from your conscience. Every child you saw bleeding can be healed. You just have to let the mind go free. Take it and let us all be free!

Odysseus takes it and puts it in his pocket.

Odysseus Tie them up.

Thoas No, I don't want to go. I want to stay here.

Dolon Typical western imperialist reactions to ideas outside the box. You can't shackle our minds, man.

Odysseus Tie them to the mast. And row!

They start to tie Dolon up. But Thoas resists.

Thoas No, please. I don't want to go. Let me stay in this place. I've never been so happy. I have found peace. Let me stay in peace! I want peace! I want peace! I want PEACE!

Thoas is fighting like a lunatic now.

Odysseus Do we have something we can give him?

Elpinor Officially, no. Unofficially . . .

Elpinor takes out a syringe.

Odysseus What is it?

Elpinor Some suppressants we've been developing. There are some long-term side-effects – manic depression, chronic suicidal tendencies, appalling nightmares. We're still fine-tuning it.

Odysseus Do it.

Elpinor injects both men. They immediately fall asleep, tied to the mast.

Elpinor One. Two. Three.

Both men wake up.

Thoas Sergeant Thoas reporting for duty.

Dolon salutes. They see how they are dressed.

Thoas Sir, I . . . I don't understand. I apologise, sir!
I have been made the victim of a pernicious prank, sir!
Permission to be untied and to dress in more suitable attire, sir!

Odysseus Permission granted. Untie him.

Thoas Dolon, follow me. Quick march!

Both men exit.

Odysseus Helmsman – head due west. Ithaca is just two weeks' sailing away!

SCENE THREE
THE CYCLOPS

The Interrogators listen agog as Odysseus continues his story.

Odysseus The Cyclops. They live without law or scruple.
They tend no crops and plant no seeds, but leave all to chance. Lone creatures haunt isolated caves in the high mountains, each one a law unto himself. And, though we did not know it then, this was the next island we came upon.

The cave of the Cyclops. Utterly dark.

Odysseus Who lives in this dark cave? I hear the sound of feet. We come in kindness, in search of hospitality and friendship. I am here with twelve of my best men to pay tribute to you and to beg you for food for our journey. We lost our provisions in a storm. The rest of my men await us back at the ships, hungry and expectant. (*He smells something.*) What's this? Cheese. It tastes good. Someone lives here.

Soldier 1 Let's take it and go back, sir. We do not need to meet the owner of the cave.

Odysseus I want to meet him. (*to the cave*) Who are you whose feet I hear in the darkness? We seek refuge and mean no harm. We bring sweet wine from the grove of Apollo as proof of our good intentions.

Sheep Baa baa baa.

Odysseus Sheep.

Soldier 1 Yes, sir.

Odysseus Well, sheep aren't frightening, are they?

Soldier 1 No sir.

Odysseus But to whom does it belong?

A mighty crash. A giant foot on hard ground.

Men. I believe at this juncture, our best strategy is to hide.

They hide. The Cyclops enters and closes the cave door. More sheep enter with him.

Sheep Baa baa baa.

Soldier 2 He has pushed a rock across the mouth of the cave. There is no way out.

The Cyclops starts to milk the sheep and goats.

Odysseus A giant man. His body as tall as the stone roof. His mouth another cave within the cave. And is it the darkness deceiving me? Or does he have just one appalling eye?

The giant, one-eyed, surveys the darkness.

Cyclops Strangers. There is no point in hiding. My one eye sees all, even in darkness. Here there is no law to protect you. There is only me and you and the justice of the cave. Tell me who you are. Why do you come sailing to this island?

Odysseus We are Greeks returning from Troy, beaten from our course by winds sent from the gods. So it is that the gods intend our visit here. Respect then our beseeching, for Zeus, the father of gods, avenges any insult suffered by suppliants and strangers.

The Cyclops laughs.

Cyclops You think you are protected by the international law of the gods here, in this darkness? I live by no rule but my own terror.

The Cyclops swoops down, grabs two of Odysseus' men, chops up their limbs and eats them.

Odysseus Ah, good gods, no! No!

Cyclops I told you, your cries are helpless. Look. Their brains are running over the ground. Clean them up, they'll stain the stone.

Two of Odysseus' men mop up the brains, in pure terror. A human leg spews out of the Cyclops' mouth.

You said you were hungry. See how kind I am? I've left you a leg. Cook it in the stone oven and eat it. Or I'll eat all of you.

Odysseus' men cook the leg in the stone oven.

Cook it on a low heat. It's tenderer. Now I want to see you eat it.

Odysseus Why does such barbarity give you pleasure?

Cyclops When you have been long enough in darkness you will see that terror is the only pleasure. Eat!

They eat, trying not to retch.

Tasty?

Soldiers Very nice. Lovely. (*Etc., etc.*)

Cyclops Wash up. I'm going to sleep. You can kill me if you want. (*He sleeps.*)

Soldier 1 He's asleep. Stab him in the chest.

Soldier 2 Stab him in the heart, in the stomach.

Odysseus No. If we kill him, we will never leave this cave but slowly die beside him. Only a giant can move that stone. That is what he wants. To deliver him from his own tyranny and condemn ourselves to death. No, my friends. We must wait upon his terror.

The Cyclops awakes and takes another two men for breakfast.

Odysseus No. No! Ah, great Zeus, why do you permit such atrocity!

Cyclops Zeus cannot hear your screams. Mop up. I will be back later. Come, sheep.

Sheep Baa baa baa.

The Cyclops opens the cave and closes it behind him.

Odysseus He has eaten four. Eight of us remain. Two he will eat for supper. That leaves six. Six of us can hold a wooden stake and pierce his eye when he is sleeping. If we fill him with wine he will not hear the sharp point until it has pierced the iris. Sharpen the stake with your knives and we will await his return.

Soldier 1 But how will we move the stone?

Odysseus Leave that to me.

The men sharpen the stake. The cave door opens.

Cyclops I'm back.

Sheep Baa baa baa.

The Cyclops and the sheep enter the cave. The Cyclops swoops down and takes two more men, swallows them whole.

Odysseus Ah ye gods! How can you permit such horror?

Cyclops Still you beseech the gods. But the gods do not dare visit here. You are in a place without hope. Now, what would you like for dinner?

Odysseus Great Cyclops, as you are eating your meal of human flesh, accompany it with some wine, fresh from the grove of Apollo. I brought it for you as a libation. See what elixir I offer you and, had you had pity on us, what benediction it could have been for you.

Cyclops You cannot but hope to dissuade me from my path. You are human. Well, give me the wine. (*He drinks it in one gulp.*) I want more. (*He drinks again.*) I want more. (*He reels. He sways.*) What is your name, you who bring nectar to emptiness? I have a gift for you too.

Odysseus My name, that my mother gave me, is Nobody.

Cyclops Nobody. My gift to you is that I will eat Nobody last, after the rest. We will eat your friends together, until at last you beg me to be killed. That will be my final victory over your soul. My head is spinning. I want to sleep. Kill me if you want. I care not. But for you, Nobody, there is no way out. (*He passes out and crashes down unconscious.*)

Odysseus Sleep, who conquers all, overcame him. As he slept, great gobbets of flesh and wine spewed out of his gullet. Watch out!

The men flee the stream of flesh and wine gurgling from the Cyclops' mouth.

We took the stake and heated it in the stone oven until it glowed.

Some god, if there are still gods in this world, give us courage!

They plunge the stake into the eye of the Cyclops.

Cyclops Aaaaaaahhhh! Treachery! My friends! Fellow Cyclops! Help me!

Voices outside the cave.

Voices Cyclops, why are you screaming?

Cyclops Good friends, Nobody is killing me!

Voices Nobody? Who is in there with you?

Cyclops Nobody!

Voices If nobody's there, why bother us at this time of night?

Cyclops But Nobody is killing me! Wait, friends! I tell you, Nobody is behind this. Nobody has tricked me, and blinded me.

Voices (*disappearing*) He's drunk. We will have to discuss his position. A Cyclops cannot show this kind of weakness.

Cyclops I tell you, Nobody is trying to destroy me!

Voices The gods will begin to think they can legislate over us – and that will be the end of our tyranny. Sad – I always thought he was the harshest of us all.

Cyclops Come back! (*He opens the stone.*) Come back!

> *Silence.*

I'll kill you. I'll take you all with me. (*The Cyclops sits across the entrance.*) Go on. Try to escape. I'll catch every one of you. I'll do unimaginable things to you. I'll make you wish for death. You'll die with me a living death without end.

Odysseus We waited as still as stone until morning. Now was the hour when the sheep go out to graze. Amongst the sheep there were some rams – tall, well-fed and seriously fleecy.

> *A very fine and large ram appears. Odysseus clings on to the underside of its belly. So do the other soldiers, each onto a large and splendid ram.*

Hold tight, men. And not a sound!

> *The first sheep goes past the Cyclops, who strokes its back.*

Cyclops There you go, my young friend.

> *The second sheep goes past the Cyclops, who strokes its back.*

Happy grazing, son.

Odysseus Each of the men passed by the Cyclops under the bellies of the rams. I came last when all the rest were free.

The ram approaches the mouth of the cave.

Cyclops Ah, my dear old ram. Why are you last leaving the cave today? It isn't like you to lag behind. Your proud strides would normally lead the flock to pasture. (*He hugs the ram.*) You would be first to drink from the running rivers, first to roll in the soft luscious grass, first to lead them back to the fold at the setting of the sun. Now you are last. Is it because you are grieving for me and my eye, branded by the evil Nobody? He is not free yet my friend. Oh, if you could tell me where he is in human voice, in what shadow he lies skulking –

Ram Baa baa baa baa.

Cyclops – I would smash his brains out on the stone floor until they daubed the walls of the cave red with my rage.

Ram Baa baa baa baa.

Cyclops I would lock his spirit in a darkness where hope never knocks.

Ram Baa. Baa. Baa! Baa!

Cyclops I know. It is frustrating. Go now. Go!

The ram leaves the cave, Odysseus still clinging on. The Cyclops is left alone.

Now the sheep are gone, Nobody. It is just you and me. I know you are in the cave somewhere. I will wait until you grow hungry and your stomach rumbles or you grow tired and your yawns betray you. Then I will find you and exercise my rage. My tyranny is more patient than your hunger. I will wait for Nobody.

Back on the ship. Two Sailors are on lookout.

Sailor Sailor, two nights have passed without sign. I fear Odysseus and his men are dead.

Sailor 2 Keep lookout. Odysseus has surprised us before.

A ram clumps aboard, Odysseus clinging on.

Ram Baa baa baa.

Sailors What is this ram doing on our ship. Shoo!

Odysseus (*from under the ram*) Do you not recognise me?

Sailors What did you say?

Odysseus (*from under the ram*) Do you not know my voice?

Sailor 1 That sounds suspiciously like our general.

Sailor 2 It can't be

Odysseus Why can't it?

Sailor 2 Oh ye gods! What have the inhabitants of this island done to great Odysseus? They have turned him into a massive ram.

Sailor 1 Call up the other men and let them witness this catastrophe.

Odysseus Wait, men. Will you still serve under me in my new shape?

Sailors Serve under you? Yes, of course. Absolutely.

Odysseus Even though I look like this?

Sailor 1 Never judge a man by his coat.

Odysseus Swear to obey me.

Sailors We will obey you, great Odysseus.

Odysseus Do you think Penelope will still agree to be my wife?

Sailor 2 What, like that? I should think so. What do you think?

Sailor 1 She should be so lucky. A ram of your stature doesn't come along every day.

Sailor 2 She'll be cock-a-hoop.

Odysseus unveils himself.

Odysseus You most faithful of men. How I rejoice in being reunited with you after my time in darkness!

Sailors Our general!

The other friends arrive under their rams.

Rams Baa baa baa.

Odysseus And here are the rest of our friends!

Sailors Friends, welcome!

Odysseus climbs the mast.

Odysseus Hear you, Cyclops! Your prisoner was not so defenceless after all! You devoured my men, you kept us locked in darkness, but your crimes will haunt you now, and the gods punish you eternally!

The Cyclops hurls rocks towards the ship. The men start to row away from the island.

He is throwing rocks at us! Ha! Who is in darkness now? Stop rowing, men! I haven't finished my tirade.

Sailors Why, hard man, are you goading him once more?
He'll shatter our ships and break our heads into pieces.

Odysseus Just stop! I want to vent my spleen.

The men stop rowing.

Odysseus Cyclops! If any man asks who has so utterly
shamed you, blinding your one eye and evading your
terror, then tell them this. It was cunning Odysseus,
sacker of cities, son of Laertes and home-maker in
Ithaca, to which he now returns unblemished and
unbowed!

Cyclops Ah now the prophecy comes true that said
I would be blinded by Odysseus. Idiot! I was on the
lookout for a great man, tall and magnificent. Instead the
gods sent a pathetic feeble creature to drink me into
destruction. Avenge my ruin, Poseidon, shaker of the
earth. Grant that Odysseus may never find home again.
Or that if he does, it shall be after intolerable suffering,
the loss of all his men, the loss of his ships and his
wealth, after years of wandering and in sheer misery.

Back in the interrogation room.

Odysseus And the god Poseidon listened and granted
that it should be so.

Beat.

Interrogator 1 Well, that's certainly a lot to chew on. I'm
going to have to take this to Head Office. Stick him in
the detention centre, Harold. We'll contact you soon.

Odysseus But you know who I am.

Interrogator 1 We know who you say you are. But
unlike your friend the Cyclops, we make sure we verify
all information received. Take him to the centre. We'll
deal with you tomorrow.

SCENE FOUR
THE DETENTION CENTRE

*Odysseus is taken to the centre. As this happens, we are
treated to the Interrogator's 'Rules and Regs' song,
accompanied by two glamorous assistants.*

Interrogator 1 The purpose of detention centres shall be
to provide SECURE but HUMANE accommodation of
detainees in a RELAXED regime.

Detainees shall enjoy as much FREEDOM of movement
and association as consistent with maintaining SAFETY
AND SECURITY.

The centre aims to encourage and assist detainees to
make the most PRODUCTIVE use of time. Respecting in
particular their DIGNITY and always being careful to
acknowledge that a human being has a legal RIGHT TO
INDIVIDUAL EXPRESSION.

The centre recognises the necessity for AWARENESS
of the particular ANXIETIES to which detainees may be
subject.

And the SENSITIVITY that this will require especially
when handling issues of racial and CULTURAL
DIVERSITY.

Every detainee shall be searched in a SEEMLY
MANNER.

Every detainee must wear CLOTHING that's suitable
and clean.

Every detainee shall have NO FOOD other than that
PROVIDED.

Every detainee shall spend an hour in the air each day.

Each detainee shall have accommodation adequate for
health.

Detainees may receive as many letters as they wish.

Detainees may receive as many visits as they wish.

The manager may with a view to ensuring the safety and security of detainees impose a prohibition on the visits to a detainee for such time as he judges right and fit.

Detainees are REQUIRED to submit to a PHYSICAL AND MENTAL examination on admittance to the centre. And the Doctor shall REPORT to his superior the case of any detainee who he suspects may be the victim of ABUSE or TORTURE.

The Doctor shall report to HIS superior the case of any detainee he suspects of having SUICIDAL OR VIOLENT THOUGHTS.

If a detainee should decease, the manager shall inform the detainee's SPOUSE OR NEXT OF KIN whenever humanly achievable.

These are the rules of the centre.
These are the rules of the centre.
These are the rules of the centre.
Thank you for your co-operation.

Odysseus alone in his room in the detention centre. He is dreaming. Penelope appears in a veil. The song resonates.

Song
These eyes are not my eyes.
This skin is not my skin.
This pale life is not my life.
Till I see my home again.
Till I see my home again.

Penelope comes close to hugging him.

Odysseus Penelope! Beautiful wife! Oh my Penelope!

A man and a woman enter suddenly and hold a knife to his throat. Odysseus awakes and Penelope disappears.

Trojan Woman Who are you?

Odysseus Don't kill me. Please don't kill me.

Trojan Man You're Greek, aren't you? Aren't you?

Odysseus No.

Trojan Man You look Greek.

Trojan Woman The last Greek here ended hanging from that pipe.

Odysseus I am not Greek.

Trojan Woman Then what are you? Where are you from?

Odysseus I have no home. I have no home, no family.

Trojan Man What is your name, stranger?

Odysseus My name. My name is Nobody.

Trojan Man Nobody. Ha ha ha. That is an excellent name. We will call you Nobody.

Trojan Woman Why are you here?

Odysseus I am a commercial traveller. The ship I was travelling on hit rocks. We were washed up here and they mistook me for an asylum seeker. I do not wish to stay in this country.

The Trojans release their grip.

Where are you from?

Trojan Woman Where do you think?

Trojan Man We are from Troy. Everyone here is from Troy.

Trojan Woman Ten years we have been wandering the world since the wooden-horse catastrophe, but no one wants us in their borders. We arrive, we plead, we sign forms, we make submissions. They keep us locked in dumps like this until they can send us somewhere else.

Trojan Man What do you sell, Nobody?

Odysseus Global paraphernalia for festivals and student towns. Perfumes. Oils. Treatments. Trinkets. Good-luck charms. Bindis and balms.

Trojan Man Drugs?

Odysseus Maybe. You want some? (*He reaches into his pocket and produces some lotus.*) Old but good.

Trojan Woman How old?

Odysseus Nine years, I think, but it still packs a punch. Try it.

Trojan Woman I don't trust you. You take some first.

Odysseus OK. Careful now. Just a little is all you need.

He takes. Pause. He smiles slightly. They take the lotus. Odysseus craftily spits his out. Pause. The Trojan Woman puts her arms round Odysseus.

Trojan Woman What did I tell you? He's a friend.

Odysseus I'm a friend, see?

Trojan Man I knew that.

Trojan Woman Did anyone ever tell you you're very beautiful?

Trojan Man Hey, this stuff is good. You know what? This detention centre is so cool! I never realised how beautifully decorated it is! It's gorgeous!

Trojan Woman Why must people go to war, Nobody?

Odysseus I have no idea.

Trojan Man Oh this lino, man, I have to feel it. And the strip lights – they're wicked, man!

Trojan Woman We're not going to war are we, Nobody?

Odysseus No.

Trojan Woman We're going to a party.

A party. Music is playing.

Trojan Woman Meet Nobody, everybody. Nobody everybody! Ha ha ha. Give them the stuff, man.

Odysseus Who are all these people?

Trojan Woman They are Trojans. They all fled the Greek army. Hand it round man! They're all our friends.

Odysseus hands round the lotus.

Odysseus Not too much now, it's my last flower.

Trojan Man Take it, man. And then I want to show you this really amazing stairwell. You see – every stair's exactly the same. Who made these stairs, man? I'm going to be a stair. Look. I'm a stair.

The partygoers take the flower. There are many partygoers (the same actors with different wigs, etc).

Trojan Woman Music! Sing with us, Nobody!

Odysseus What do you sing?

Trojan Woman We can sing whatever we want.

Trojan Man We can say whatever we want.

Trojan Woman And we'll tell you why.

35

They sing the Trojan song.

Trojans
A Trojan can say that her mother was killed
By a vicious militia of vitamin pills.
She can say she was raped by a lemon soufflé ,
'Cos no one believes us whatever we say.

A Trojan can say that his city was sacked
By a Siamese cat who attacked and attacked
And the kittens were shooting a family a day,
'Cos no one believes us whatever we say.

Chorus
We say baa baa baa baa we say boo boo boo boo
We say nee nee nee nee and then fam fam faroo
We say ha ha ha ha and hee hee hee
We say no one believes us whatever we say.

I told them my country was burnt to the ground
By a man who wore glasses that were perfectly round.
I said that a fish took my sister away,
'Cos no one believes me whatever I say.

I said I was whipped by an army of Greeks.
I said I was stripped by a squadron of leeks.
I said that my children were squashed by a tray,
'Cos no one believes me whatever I say.

We say baa baa baa baa we say boo boo boo boo
We say nee nee nee nee and then fam fam faroo
We say ha ha ha ha and hee hee hee
We say no one believes us whatever we say
Yes no one believes us whatever we say.

Odysseus I believe you. I am Nobody and I believe you!

Trojans
We say baa baa baa we say boo boo boo
We say nee nee nee and then fam fam faroo

36

We say ha ha ha ha and hee hee hee
We say no one believes us whatever we say
Yes no one believes us whatever we say!

The dance continues. Odysseus is dancing with a girl,
Maira.

Maira That's good stuff you brought, where did you get
it?

Odysseus That would be telling.

Maira Oh go on.

Odysseus I got it from an island of lotus eaters on my
way to meet a giant Cyclops with one eye.

Maira A likely story. And I doubt your name's really
Nobody either. I feel like I know you from somewhere.

Odysseus I don't think so.

Maira How come you speak our language?

Odysseus I had business in Troy once.

Maira Maybe I saw you there.

Odysseus It was long ago. You would have been a child.
What's your name?

Maira Maira.

Odysseus You look happy, Maira.

Maira That's thanks to you and your magic herb.

Trojan Freaky!! If you stare at the security cameras long
enough – they start to look like monsters!

Maira Oh Nobody . . . sometimes I want to shake
people so hard their eyes would fall out of their sockets.

She leans against him. The dancing has faded.

If I could stay here for ever in your arms I would.

Odysseus You're high.

Maira Yup.

Trojans A song, Maira. Sing that song!

Maira I'm too busy hugging this gorgeous stranger.

Trojans Go on, sing!

Maira Oh, all right.

> This room is not my room.
> This bed is not my own.
> This pale bulb is not my dawn.
> This home is not my home.
>
> These walls are not my walls.
> This dream is not my own.
> This pale breath is not my breath.
> This home is not my home.

Odysseus It was you singing that song. The song that makes me weep for home. It was you.

Maira I thought you didn't have a home.

Odysseus Sing it again. Please sing it.

Maira
> These eyes are not my eyes.
> This skin is not my skin.
> This pale life is not my life.
> Till I see my home again.
> Till I see my home again.

> *Odysseus cries.*

SCENE FIVE
CIRCE

The interrogation room. The two Interrogators listening.

Odysseus Fleeing the curse of the Cyclops, we sailed with our six ships to the isle where Aeolus lived, a gracious man with six sons and six daughters.

Aeolus stands with six sons and six daughters.

Aeolus Odysseus, you have feasted well. It is time for you to depart. Take this bag of oxen hide. Inside it are all the blowing winds. Zeus made me their guardian to have them rise and fall at my pleasure. Now you take them and control them so that you shall no longer be blown from your course. Keep this bag secret – do not tell your men what is inside, for their curiosity will overwhelm them. But I will first set the West Wind free to carry you on your way and set you fair for home.

Aeolus opens the bag of winds and releases the West Wind, which sings.

West Wind Aaaah. Aaaah. Aaaah. Aaaah.

On the ship. Odysseus holds the bag of winds.

Odysseus We set sail. I held tight to the bag, and would let no man know what it was or why I had been given it. But I grew and sleep overcame me. That was when Poseidon entered the minds of my men with his treachery.

Soldier 1 Look. Even sleep favours him.

Soldier 2 He is loved by everyone, bestowed with gifts, showered with honours. He'll return home laden with the riches plundered from Troy. What do we get?

Soldier 1 We fought as hard. Suffered as much. We've been through the same trials and tribulations. We deserve equal pickings!

Soldier 2 And now he's got a little bonus. That bag under his arm. The old man gave it him on the island when we weren't looking. What jewels must be in there!

Soldier 1 Silver and gold!

Soldier 3 Diamonds and pearls!

Soldier 2 That's why he won't tell us what's inside. He wants it all for himself.

Soldier 1 Let's get it off him.

They tickle Odysseus' arm until he releases the bag.

Soldier 1 What do we do now?

Soldier 2 Open it. We have a right to that bounty same as him.

Soldier 3 But he forbade it.

Soldier 2 Of course he did. Let's find out why.

They open the bag. Blackout.

The island of Circe. A massive shipwreck. Odysseus raises his head.

Odysseus Five of our ships sunk. Just our own broken boat remaining. Almost all the men dead. And us few remaining blown to the farthest point of the compass. Starving. Shattered. Ah, the folly of man!

Elpinor I can see smoke, sir.

Odysseus What godforsaken island is this? What new trial do the gods have in store for us? We no longer know where is the sun and where the darkness. Go and investigate. Take half the men. I'll wait for you here.

Elpinor and his men carefully approach the smoke. They hear a beautiful woman singing.

Circe La la la la. La la la la la la la. La la la la. La la la la la la la.

Elpinor What a bewitching tune.

Soldier 1 Smell that smell.

Soldier 2 Warm meats.

Eurylochos Soft melting cheese.

Elpinor Baking bread

Soldier 1 Pale honey

Eurylochos Barley wine

Circe appears, surrounded by tame lions and wolves.

Circe Come and feast, soldiers. It's all ready for you.

Soldier 2 Such beauty.

Soldier 1 Her hair.

Elpinor Her soft skin. The curve of her breasts.

Soldier 1 And the lions and the wolves fawning on her like gentle lovers.

Eurylochos Hold on. I don't trust it. Only black magic can achieve this.

Soldier Oh, Eurylochos.

Circe Come in, strangers. (*She enters.*)

Eurylochos No, it's too delicious. My mother used to warn me about women like her.

Soldier Stay outside then, if you're so worried.

Eurylochos I think I will.

The others enter. Eurylochos listens up close to the shining doors.

Circe Eat, my friends. Eat and drink and when you are finished I shall entertain you. All of you.

Eurylochos She's putting a secret potion in the sweet wine. They didn't see her do it. Oh my friends, do not drink!

The sound of a great drinking. The sound of a great eating.

Soldiers We are finished, goddess.

Circe Now for your entertainment.

Eurylochos She's opening her gown. They're all staring at her naked body. She's taking a wand from the inside pocket of the gown. Stop, men. Stop! She's going to strike you with the wand!

A strike. Pause. The sound of pigs. Pigs scuttle over the stage.

Eurylochos Men! My friends, comrades. What has happened to you?

Pigs Haw haw haw.

Eurylochos Silas? Is that you? Calchon? Elpinor?

Pigs Haw haw haw.

Eurylochos Odysseus!

Eurylochos runs out.

Pigs
Haw haw haw.
Haw haw haw.
Haw haw haw.

Circe enters.

Circe Come, my trotters. Into your sty. And eat shit.

The ship. Eurylochos runs in.

Eurylochos Odysseus. You have to . . . they've all been turned into . . . haw haw haw . . .

Odysseus Talk sense, man!

Eurylochos A naked goddess has turned your men into pigs!

The goddess Athena appears.

Athena Odysseus. Go alone to the goddess Circe. But first take this herb. It will protect you from the day of evil. She will put drugs in your food but this antidote will keep you from harm. When she goes to strike you with her wand, attack her, threaten to kill her, and she will be afraid and ask you to go to bed with her. Do not refuse her invitation.

Eurylochos You won't find that a problem.

Athena For through your love she will set your friends free and reinvigorate your journey home.

Eurylochos and Odysseus approach the house.

Circe (*singing*) La la la la. La la la la la la la. La la la la.
La la la la la la la.

Odysseus The smells. Barley. Warm meats. Soft melting
cheese. Baking bread.

Eurylochos Yes, I know. Pale honey. Barley wine. Can
we just get on with it. You go in. I'll wait out here.

Odysseus Coward.

Eurylochos Imperialist.

*Odysseus takes the herb. Eurylochos hides. Circe
enters.*

Circe Come and feast, stranger. It's all laid out for you.

They enter.

Eurylochos She's giving him the wine. Yes, she's putting
in the potion. He drinks deeply. She smiles. He tucks into
some roasted lamb and soft melted feta. She strokes his
head. He dips his finger into the pale honey and licks it.
She invites him towards her. She opens her gown. He
takes in her body in great gulps. She presses his honeyed
lips to her bare thighs. She takes the wand from the
inside pocket and . . .

Circe Now go to your sty and join your friends!

*Circe screams. Odysseus and Circe tear out of the
house. Odysseus has a knife to Circe's throat.
Eurylochos hides.*

What man are you? What city are you from? You drink
my drug-steeped wine but are not enchanted. You have a
mind immune to my magic. You must be the cunning
Odysseus.

Odysseus How do you know?

Circe I was told you would come by the god Hermes. Be calm, warrior. Put down your knife and climb with me to my bed. In lying together we will have faith and trust in each other.

Odysseus Circe, it is hard for me that you ask me to be so gentle with you when you have turned my men into pigs and tried to do the same to me. Swear then, goddess, that you will do me no further harm when I am naked. Swear and I will lie with you.

Circe I swear. I will love you with abandon and when you wish to leave, you will be free to do so. Now come, warrior. Come.

> *They climb into Circe's bed. Circe removes her gown and the love-making begins.*

Eurylochos And so Odysseus mounted the surpassingly beautiful bed of the goddess Circe. The bastard.

Circe La la la la. La la la la la la la. La la la la. La la la la la la la

Pigs Haw haw haw. Haw haw haw.

> *The chorus of love-making and pigs snorting rises to a glorious crescendo.*

> *Interval.*

Act Two

SCENE SIX

Interrogator 1 dashes in.

Interrogator 1 Listen. Listen. Pipe down, will ya? Listen
– how was your drink, was it all right? Good – listen,
I've nipped in early because, well to be honest I've flat
had enough of this. I mean it's all one-way traffic, isn't
it? Odysseus this, Odysseus that. I know it's called the
bleeding *Odyssey*, but what about my side of the story?
I'm not saying it should be called *The Rogerssey*. I can
see that lacks the same resonance. But you've got to have
balance. Thing about writers – they've always got to
have a slant. This one's gooey liberal. Poor little helpless
foreigners, that's his take. Well, he doesn't have to fight
on the firing line. The number of people coming through
here with diseases, mental illness, addiction, history of
violence. I'd like to see him try the caring-sharing
fucking approach with them. Then there's all the
nationalities. They're all different, and they all need a
different treatment. The Minoans, they're always down
in the dumps. Sort of melancholic, dunno why. So I try a
joke with them, stop them taking themselves so seriously.
Your Mesopotamians on the other hand tend to be
psychopathic, so keep it formal, no time for a laugh with
them. Spartans – tough violent bastards – always have at
least two men in the room. Persians – smooth as silk but
don't trust 'em, they'll have the skin off your back.
Phoenicians – cunning little devils. Beautiful women.
Which is part of their cunning. Very beautiful. There was
one particular Phoenician woman. She quite stole my
heart, as it happens. Yeah, well. That's another story. She

46

was brought in, right. She didn't say much at first. But she had the most beautiful eyes I had ever seen. And dark dark hair. Anyway, she started to talk a bit. In a way it was the usual story – civil war, family dead, no one left in the world. But I was all at sea, I was quite unable to exercise my normal professional control. The session was ending, and there was so much that hadn't been said. I just wanted her to know she wasn't alone. I kissed her. Her initial reaction obviously was one of acute distress. I was horrified, said I'd leave her, get her someone else, a female counsellor – due process and all – anyway she calmed down a bit and she asked me to stay. Well by now the interview was way over time but I didn't care. We just sat and she talked, I kept my distance, but I could see that she was inching her chair towards me, inching it, you know, and I'm, like, stay calm Roger, and she's inching and I'm bricking it inside. Until we're side by side. And then . . . well, my heart explodes when I think about it. She held my hand. She was holding it and tears in her eyes, and I know time is seriously up, and I think to myself she's never going to be let in. She's got no evidence to prove anything. Left in too much of a hurry to get it. So I say to her – I'll get you out. I'll help you disappear. I mean, this is not normal Roger Dawson behaviour, trust me. But we arrange it. I'll pick her up from the detention centre that night under some pretence or other and I'll 'lose' her in transit. It happens. We arrange a time. She makes me promise not to let her down. I arrive at the detention centre. They won't let me in. 'You've been taken off the case, Dawson.' They must have picked up on something. I'm desperate to get a message to her. They won't take it. They say come in the morning and leave it then. I come back in the morning. People are looking funny. I ask why the sad faces. They say . . . they say . . . there's a girl been found hanging . . . in the ladies' . . . from her shoelaces . . . And that's why I always tell young Harold: never get too involved!

Where were we? Oh yeah, Circe's palace.

Exit. Circe's palace. Circe and Odysseus lie in her bed.

Odysseus La la la la. La la la la la la la. La la la la. La la la la la la la.

Enter four Maidservants, singing.

Maidservants
I bring the covers, as purple as dusk,
I bring the bowls, of elephant tusk,
I bring the wine, so fragrant and sweet,
And I bring the water to tickle her feet.

We are the servants of Circe
Cir-Cir-Circe we serve
Circe we serve
We are the servants of Circe
Cir-Cir-Circe we serve
Circe we serve.

I bring the oils to pamper her skin,
I bring the blankets, to snuggle her in,
I bring the henna to burnish her hair,
And I bring the cushions to rumple her chair.

We are the servants of Circe
Cir-Cir-Circe we serve
Circe we serve
We are the servants of Circe
Cir-Cir-Circe we serve
Circe we serve.

Chorus and repeats.

She's coming down! She's bringing the warrior! Quick, girls.

Odysseus and Circe descend and are oiled and pampered by the Maidservants.

Circe Enough. Leave us to feast alone. We have a hunger on us.

The Maidservants depart. Circe eats ravenously, but Odysseus desists.

Cat got your tongue? Why do you sit eating your heart out but touch neither food nor drink? Do you still suspect me? You have nothing to fear.

Odysseus How can I touch a morsel of this feast when I know my friends are still stuck in that sty? If you want me to eat and drink, set them free.

We hear a distant grunting. Circe rises, takes her wand and opens the door of the pigsty. The pigs come running out.

Pigs Haw haw haw.
Haw haw haw.

Circe blesses them. They transform one by one into men until there is only one pig left, Elpinor.

Soldiers Where am I? Odysseus! General! What happened to us?

They see the remaining pig.

Soldiers Oh, look at that little pig. Aaah. Sweet. By the way, where's Elpinor?

They all suddenly remember.

Soldiers Oh God. Oh no. That isn't . . .

Odysseus That's Elpinor.

Soldiers Does that mean . . . we were . . . oh my god. Is that really Elpinor? Hello, Elpinor, me old mucker. Pig of a day, isn't it? (*Etc.*)

Elpinor Haw haw haw.

Odysseus Release him, Circe.

Circe releases him.

Elpinor Master! What happened to me?

Odysseus But Elpinor! You look taller, and more attractive than before. Now I think of it, so do all you men.

Soldiers Do we? Do I? Yes, you do. You're gorgeous. You too, mate. Thanks. (*Etc.*)

Odysseus Is this your work?

Circe It's the least I can do to make up for my anger. Now, let us feast!

Odysseus For a year we feasted with the divine Circe, and every night I slept in her high bed with her exquisite body beside me. But too much even of the finest wine palls. So my thoughts crept back to home. And Circe noticed my mind showing my body the way to wander.

Circe kisses Odysseus.

Circe Your heart is no longer in your kisses. Well, I will keep my promise. You shall not stay in this house against your will. But your journey will not be easy for you are now so out of your way. Your path home must be through the land of the dead, the house of Hades and Persephone. You must find the grove beyond the ocean, where poplars grow and the two rivers pour into Acheron by the great rock. There you must dig the pit to invite those from the land of the dead. Pour libations of milk, wine and honey. Add water and sprinkle with barley. Then sacrifice a black sheep and a white ram. Pour their blood into the pit and the dead will come. Among them, find Tiresias, the blind seer, whose senses alone remain awake within him. He will help you. The gods dictate that this is the only way.

Odysseus weeps.

Odysseus My heart does not wish to go on longer. But I must go on.

My heart does not wish to see sunlight again. But I must see it.

Is this the only way, to broach the impregnable land of the dead, where no ship has ever ventured?

Circe It is the only way.

Song
　These eyes are not my eyes.
　This skin is not my skin.
　This pale life is not my life.
　Till I see my home again.
　Till I see my home again.

SCENE SEVEN
THE LAND OF THE DEAD

Odysseus at the gateway to the land of the dead.

Odysseus This is the gateway to the dead. Here is the grove dotted with black poplars. There is the great rock, where the two rivers flow into Acheron. I must dig a pit here.

Odysseus digs a pit.

Now pour in the libations. First honey with milk. Now sweet wine. Now water. Sprinkle with barley. Now I must take the blood of the black ewe and the white ram, pour it into the pit.

He pours the blood of the sheep into the pit.

The souls of the dead appear, sensing the blood.
They try to approach.

Odysseus All the legions of dead are here before me.
Brides, young unmarried warriors, wizened elders and
tender virgins with sorrow in their hearts. Faces I recognise
from the battlefields of Troy. Their cheeks once filled
with the blood of war. Now as hollow as caves. Their
empty eyes stare on the blood as death looks on life.
Keep back from me! You shall not taste the blood! You
must help me first, dead souls. Tell me – where is blind
Tiresias?

The ghouls gesture to an old man. Odysseus allows
him forward to drink from the blood of the sheep.
This is Tiresias.

Tiresias Son of Laertes and seed of Zeus, why, unhappy
man, have you shunned the light and come here to look
on dead men? Why come to this joyless place?

Odysseus Circe instructed me and I came.

Tiresias You seek a sweet homecoming. But the gods
will not make it easy. Poseidon has it in for you. Still you
might make it, after much suffering, if you can control
your desires and those of your men.

Odysseus How do I control them?

Tiresias You will soon enough reach the cattle of the
sun – ripe, fine animals that chew grass on the slopes
of a sun-kissed isle. If you leave these blessed beasts
untouched, you and your men will make it to Ithaca
unharmed. But if your friends so much as touch one of
these sacred cattle, I prophesy destruction to them and to
your ship. And you, Odysseus, will come home as a piece
of wrecked driftwood, quite desolate, in a stranger's boat
and with nothing but your own skin.

Odysseus This is as the gods themselves have spun it.

Tiresias Before you go. Look behind you.

Odysseus looks behind him. Odysseus' Mother stands there.

Odysseus Tiresias, the dead soul I see before me is my own mother. Is it not?

Tiresias It is.

Odysseus My mother has died in my absence and I did not know. Mother, why do you sit next to the blood in silence, and why do you not even look at me, your own son? Tiresias, help me. What will make her know I am here?

Tiresias Allow her to drink of the blood. Then she will know you and give you true answer. I will leave you. (*He leaves.*)

Odysseus Drink, Mother. Drink.

Odysseus' Mother drinks. She sees Odysseus and weeps.

Mother My child! How have you pierced this fog being still alive? You are still alive?

Odysseus I am alive.

Mother To reach this darkness is hard for the living. The rivers are wide and deep and the ocean terrible, but you are here. You are come from Troy?

Odysseus I am returning from there.

Mother But you have not yet reached home? Not seen your wife?

Odysseus Not yet. I came here for that purpose. To consult Tiresias. For I cannot get near Greece or any of its islands, nor can I set foot on any dry land, but have endured agony after agony, pursued by the furious gods. But tell me, how did you die? Was it a long sickness? Did you suffer? And tell me of my father, my son, my wife? Is she still faithful despite everything? Does she still wait for me?

Mother She waits for you and wastes away her days and nights with weeping. Your son, just a babe in arms when you left, is now a man, albeit one who has never known his father. He does his best to maintain rule and keep the dogs from the palace. Your father never visits the city. He sleeps in winter in the stables on the estate without blankets or bedclothes, and in summer he lies grieving in the orchard. He longs for your return and age wears harshly on him. And so it was with me. I did not die of sickness, but, my shining boy, of longing for you, your cleverness and your gentle ways. That was what took my spirit from me.

Odysseus Oh, Mother. Mother. Oh, my mother.

Odysseus tries to hold his mother but he cannot. Her shape disappears from his grasp.

Mother. Let me hold you. (*He tries again.*) Mother! (*He tries again.*)

Mother It is not possible. You must go back to the light.

Odysseus But when I get home. What will happen when I get home?

Mother When you get home, this sight will greet you.

Penelope is surrounded by suitors, who are almost ravishing her.

Your wife assailed on all sides by bad men, her honour under threat, her fidelity tested to the limit. You will punish these men, kill them with your arrow and drive the evil from your land.

Odysseus Show me.

The old swineherd appears.

Mother There look. The old swineherd Eumaeus. Join him. He is taking you into your own home.

Enter to Penelope and the suitors, Odysseus and Eumaeus, an old man. Odysseus in rags. The suitors laugh. Antinoos, the worst, speaks.

Antinoos Old man, why do you bring this tramp into the palace? Haven't we got enough trouble as it is with the homeless littering the streets without bringing them in here?

Old Man This was not well-spoken, Antinoos. A beggar more than any other needs hospitality. But you, worst of men, are only interested in filling your own stomach. And this is not even your house!

Antinoos What are you saying, you ungrateful swineherd? You're lucky to have a job at all. Bringing vermin to our hearth!

Odysseus Sir. I also know what it is to sit and eat in a great house. I lived in one once, just like this one before me. Often I gave to passing vagabonds. So should you now. That piece of bread in your hand would not cost you much.

Antinoos This piece, you mean? This piece here? (*He eats it.*) No, it wouldn't cost me much. Now get out before I kick you back to whatever godforsaken stone you crawled from.

Penelope Antinoos, is this how to impress me as a suitor? Give food to this stranger I implore you. Unfortunate man, forced to walk the streets begging alms. His helplessness is to be pitied.

Antinoos I'll show him pity.

He throws the footstool at Odysseus. They laugh.

Penelope Enough. Is it not enough that you spend every day here in my husband's house? Is it not enough that you eat up the substance of a man whose bones lie festering under a foreign sky? Get out.

Antinoos Soon one of us will be giving the orders.

The suitors depart.

Mother She does not recognise you. You must talk to her.

Odysseus Sweet lady, I thank you for your kindness.

Penelope Where do you hail from, sir?

Odysseus Do not ask me this. Question me on any other matter, but do not ask who I am, the name of my country. My heart may break with the telling.

Penelope You can cry all you like, your tears will dissolve in the ocean of my own. My heart is wasting away with longing for my husband, twenty years gone, dead maybe, who can say? These men try to force me to remarry. My parents want me to make a match for the good of the country. I have held out for so many years. I waste away at the inward heart. My resistance is at an end. I feel I know you from somewhere. I talk to you so easily. I ask again, who are you?

Odysseus I am a soldier.

Penelope Of whose army? Of whose army?

Odysseus Of Odysseus' army.

Penelope You knew my husband?

Odysseus And know him still. He is alive, and will be here soon.

Penelope If only what you say were true! But my heart tells me differently. He is dead to me, and for me, and in me.

Odysseus Then if you wish to see him return from the dead, this is what you must do.

Penelope rises.

Penelope Listen to me, proud suitors! You have used my home as an alehouse long enough! You have wolfed my food and gulped my wine. All in competition for my hand. Well, now is the time. Here is the bow of great Odysseus. There are the twelve axes. He who can string the bow and send an arrow through the axes will be worthy of Odysseus' place in my bed. That man, and no other, will marry me, and take me away from this place of memories for ever.

One of the suitors, Leodes, steps up.

Leodes Let me try! I have been a bowman all my life. I will easily shatter the axes and claim my bride. (*But when he tries to string the bow he fails.*) I can't even string it! It's impossible! Impossible, I say!

Antinoos Let me try, Leodes, you're such a waste of space. My bride-to-be, I salute you. The rest – watch and learn. (*But he cannot string the bow. The bow escapes him.*) Come on, you . . . come here I say! I'll master you. Come on now! (*Finally he hurls the bow down in frustration.*) That is not a bow. It is a devil!

Odysseus Dear friends, let me try the bow, so I may find out what strength remains in my poor fingers.

The suitors laugh.

Leodes You? You couldn't string a child's bow!

Antinoos Haven't you insulted us enough, coming into our house, begging for our food, drinking our wine! Get the message. You don't belong here!

Penelope It is not your house, Antinoos. Not your wine. Not your food. Let him try.

> *Odysseus strings the bow and sends it through the twelve axes. But when he turns to claim Penelope she is gone. Instead his mother stands there and we are back in the land of the dead.*

Mother You will live in peace with Penelope. But only if you get home. Remember Tiresias' warning. Do not eat of the cattle of the sun. (*She turns to leave.*)

Odysseus Mother.

Mother Go back to the light.

Odysseus Mother!

Mother Back to the light. (*She recedes into darkness.*)

Odysseus Mother! Mother!!

SCENE EIGHT
ODYSSEUS' WANDERINGS:
THE CATTLE OF THE SUN

We are in the interrogation room.

Interrogator 1 Yeah? And?

Odysseus And what?

Interrogator 2 What happened next?

Odysseus You can guess what happened next.

Interrogator 2 No we can't. You got to tell us.

Odysseus You can't even understand me!

Interrogator 2 I can! Roger's been teaching me.

Odysseus In three days?

Interrogator 2 I'm a fast learner!

Odysseus You know enough. Either give me passage home or throw me out on the street. I'll find my own way.

Interrogator 1 Sit down. Sit down! Now listen, Head Office are aware of the uniqueness of your case. They've taken it to the top. We're expecting a decision any minute. But you got to give us the whole story! I can't submit the application without a decent ending. They'll chuck it right back at my face.

Odysseus suddenly grabs both men by the neck and pins them down on the table.

Odysseus Do you not hear what I say? I have had enough!

Interrogator 1 That's all very well but it won't wash with the authorities!

Odysseus releases them.

And besides, Harold here – tell him Harold. About your lad.

Interrogator 2 Yeah, well, my boy, right. He's eight, right. Well, he loves all the adventure stories, fantasy games and all that. So I've been telling him a bit about you.

Interrogator 1 You've been telling him the stories is what you've been doing. What's his favourite?

Interrogator 2 Cyclops. Yeah.

Interrogator 1 You see? This is bigger than just you and me, mate. Harold junior's waiting back at home with bated breath.

Interrogator 2 And his mates too. He's told them all and they've got their dads to tell the stories back to them. They've even got stickers.

Interrogator 1 You see what I'm saying? You got to finish it off. It's just the cattle of the sun, which, seeing as you're here, I'm guessing didn't go that well, and we're home and dry. What do you say? There's a boat back to Ithaca in it for you.

Odysseus I get an answer tonight?

Interrogator 1 You get an answer tonight. And I'm telling ya, between you, me and the doorpost, it's looking positive.

Odysseus rises from his chair.

You just put a smile on one nipper's face.

Odysseus We left the land of the dead and after one more night with the divine Circe sailed towards home. The great goddess blessed us with a strong wind that filled the sails. We made fast the tackling and let the helmsman steer us across the great ocean. But then I remembered what Circe had whispered in my ear as we lay enfolded in each other's arms.

Circe On your journey home you will come first of all to the sirens, enchanters of mortal men. He who hears the sirens unprepared and unsuspecting has no chance of reaching home and delighting wife and child, for he will be snared by their sublime song. They sit singing in a meadow but the beach before them is piled high with the

bones of men who succumbed, now rotted away, their
skins shrivelled to dust. You must drive on past them.
Melt down some honey wax and stuff it in your men's
ears so none can listen. But if you yourself fancy hearing
it, then have them tie you hand and foot to the mast so
that you may have your joy. The more you cry out to be
set free to lose yourself in that irresistible music, the
harder your men, deaf to your cries, must row and the
tighter your binds must be tied until you are out of the
reach of that melodious poison.

Odysseus is tied to the mast. Hands and feet.

Odysseus We are approaching the island of the Sirens.
On my order place the honey wax in your ears and row!
Do not stop, whatever my silent cries, however frenzied
my attempts to break free. Your failure will mean
destruction to us all. (*Pause.*) Now.

*All the Sailors put the honey wax in. As they do so,
silence pours across the stage. Odysseus is still talking
but we do not hear him. Now the music is clearly
upon us, for Odysseus is knocked back and swoons,
his body racked with spasms of ecstasy. He starts to
break at the ropes, but they are tied tighter by the
men. He screams and shouts, 'Turn back, turn back,'
he rails and he rants. But no sound issues. Now his
screaming begins to fade and he is weeping,
wrenching his guts in volleys of tears.*

    *The men, as one, remove the honey wax. The sound
of the sea returns, but no music.*

You bastards! You scum, you utter filth, I'll kill you all,
you fascists, you life-hating, love-murdering fascist sons
of bitches. Turn back. Please. Please. Turn back! Turn
back!

Sailors But your home, general. Your wife.

Odysseus Fuck my wife! Fuck my home! Turn back. Oh ye gods, please make them turn back, turn back, turn back . . .

The men row on quietly across the ocean.

The island of the cattle of the sun. Odysseus is asleep, still tied to the mast. The men sit and wait for his awakening. And so he wakes.

Odysseus How long have I slept?

Sailors Many days.

Odysseus Untie me now. What land is this, Elpinor?

Elpinor This is Thrinakia. Home to the cattle of the sun.

Odysseus The cattle of the sun. But have you remembered Tiresias' prophecy? If we eat the cattle we are doomed to destruction!

Elpinor We haven't touched them, general. Eurylochos wanted to but I remembered Tiresias' prophecy.

Eurylochos I didn't suggest we ate them. I merely observed how plump and succulent they look.

Odysseus If we are aware of the destruction they will cause, then why are we here, tempting fate? Let us leave immediately.

Elpinor The winds died, my general, just as we reached the island. The currents are too strong for our oars. We have been stranded here for three days already.

Odysseus Well, we have food and drink stored on ship. So we can eat that and wait for the winds to revive. Do not even touch the cattle. They belong to the sun, who sees everything. I will watch over you to ensure no man weakens. We will wait for the wind.

Dawn came with rosy fingers. Still no wind. We ate the salted meats and the wine.

Dawn came with rosy fingers. No wind. We polished off the jars of herring, the pickled fruits and the anchovies.

Three more rosy-fingered dawns. We forced down the fish paste and the dried biscuits.

A month more. We had not eaten for five days. Still no wind! Why is there still no wind?

Men, I will go alone on to the island to hunt for fish and permitted meat. The rest of you stay on the beach. Do not so much as set foot into the green fields before you.

Odysseus stumbles out into the fields.

Great Zeus, all you gods who hold Olympus, have mercy on me! My men are dying, bereft of wind, bereft of hope, they can go no further under this harsh condition you set upon us. Bring us respite, great gods, for your justice is hard, implacable and incomprehensible to me. (*He prays but is filled with a deep tiredness.*) Why am I sleepy? Why is this slumber falling upon me now, when I can least afford it? Dear gods, why? (*He falls into a slumber.*)

Back on the boat.

Elpinor I don't understand it. He hasn't returned.

Eurylochos He's probably caught himself a nice juicy rabbit and is roasting it on an open fire.

Sailor 1 Or a carp fresh from a running river.

Sailor 2 Or a giant crab grabbed from a rocky shore.

Eurylochos Meanwhile we sit and starve. Friends, what worse death is there than hunger? These fatted cows sit before us in that field to taunt us with their milk and meat. Look at them, gorgeous fleshy devils. Let us take the finest we can see, squeeze out its milk and cut its throat, sacrificing it humbly to the gods as we do, and when we return to Ithaca we'll build a temple in honour of the sun god to keep him happy. And if Circe is right and this action condemns us, so what? I would rather die gulped down by the waves than waste slowly to nothing on this miserable shore.

Sailors I agree! Agreed!

Elpinor But did you not hear the words of our general?

Eurylochos You have been too faithful too long, Elpinor. Let's find the fattest cow in the herd! Which one do you fancy?

Sailors I like the look of that one. Here's a cracker! (*Etc.*)

> *They enter the audience.*

> *Back on the island a wind is blowing. Odysseus awakes.*

Odysseus A wind. A wind. Men! Men! Men! (*He runs, galloping, leaping, sprinting. But then stops dead.*) What is this smell that wafts on the breeze? Dear gods, let it not be so! Zeus, how could you lull me into dreams as this monstrosity was perpetuated?

> *He sees the men tucking great slabs of cooked beef into their mouths. Elpinor amongst them.*

Odysseus You heathens! What have you done? Who tempted you to such self-destruction?

Sailor 1 It wasn't me.

Sailor 2 Nor me.

Eurylochos It was Elpinor.

Elpinor No, my lord, I argued against it, but was overswayed.

Odysseus Overswayed? Do you know what destruction you have wrought upon us? Quick, back to the boat. Maybe you have not eaten enough for the punishment to be as harsh as threatened. Put sail straightaway and take not a morsel of meat with you!

They up and leave, but Eurylochos pockets a sliver of red flesh.

Sailors Hoist the mainsail, trisail and the topsail. Fasten the tackle! Hoist anchor!

The boat sets to sea.

Odysseus The sky is blue. The wind is firm but not fierce. No storm clouds threaten the horizon. Dear gods, have mercy on us and our too-human hunger. Have mercy on this three-year journey of pain, and lead us home!

Odysseus prays. The men pray, but Eurylochos sneaks a bit of beef into his mouth. The sky erupts.

Oh ye gods! Why do you forsake us?

The mast falls. Eurylochos is swept overboard.

Eurylochos Help! Help!

Sailors
Night springs from heaven.
Ship on the current flies
Sail shreds into seven
Wind spits in our eyes.

The Sailors are swept overboard. Sails crash.

General! Elpinor! Help me!

Night springs from heaven.
Ship on the current flies
Sail shreds into seven
Wind spits in our eyes.

Elpinor is swept overboard.

Elpinor General! Odysseus!

Odysseus Elpinor! Take my hand!

Elpinor The current is too strong.

Odysseus Elpinor! Faithful Elpinor!

Elpinor Odysseus, find home. Kiss the sweet soil of Ithaca for Elpinor.

Odysseus Elpinor! Elpinor!

Elpinor disappears beneath the waves. A dark cloud rises and engulfs the scene.

Odysseus wakes and pulls himself from a piece of shattered sail. The goddess Calypso sits staring at him.

Odysseus Who are you?

Calypso I am the goddess Calypso. You have been washed up alone on my shore. All of your men are dead. Now you must stay with me awhile.

Odysseus How long? How long must I stay, ye vengeful gods?

In the interrogation room.

Interrogator 1 How long? How long did you stay?

Odysseus Seven years.

Interrogator 2 Christ.

Odysseus Then Hermes came and ordered her to set me free. She gave me a raft, sent me homewards. But Poseidon was not finished. He wrecked the raft and hurled me on your shore where you found me, naked and bereft. And that is the end of my story.

Pause.

Interrogator 1 Take him back to the centre, Harold. We'll have an answer tonight.

SCENE NINE
THE TROJAN HORSE

Another party is in progress. They sing.

I said that my girlfriend had been disappeared
After meeting a man with a mighty long beard
And her body was found in a chicken satay
'Cos no one believes me whatever I say.

I said that my family was locked in a shed
By a violent priest who had seventy heads.
I said that the heads made us kneel down and pray,
'Cos no one believes us whatever we say.

Chorus:
We say baa baa baa baa we say boo boo boo boo
We say nee nee nee nee and then fam fam faroo
We say ha ha ha ha and hee hee hee
'Cos no one believes us whatever we say.

I said I that I fled from a goose with a gun
Who was flapping his feathers and eating a bun.
I said that he honked as I sprinted away,
'Cos no one believes me whatever I say.

I said that the sky lies just under the ground.
I said hell was above and that heaven was down.
I said that it's nice in Guantanamo Bay,
'Cos no one believes us whatever we say.

We say baa baa baa baa we say boo boo boo boo
We say nee nee nee nee and then fam fam faroo
We say ha ha ha ha and hee hee hee
Nobody believes us whatever we say.

Odysseus, in buoyant spirits, is dragged in.

Trojan Man Come on Nobody, join us!

Odysseus You lot are always having parties.

Trojan Woman What else is there to do? Have a drink.

Odysseus I will. I'm in the mood to celebrate. I may
have good news tonight.

Trojan Woman Let the lucky laugh and the unlucky
drink. (*She drinks*.) Now be honest. Do you have any
more of that flower?

Odysseus All gone. I swear! I gave the last of it to
Maira.

Trojan Woman Ah well, it will be all gone then.

Odysseus Where is she?

Trojan Woman She is preparing a show. You must stay
to watch it.

Odysseus I may be called away. I may be leaving
tonight.

Trojan Man Be our guest until then. We will not be offended.

The story begins.

Trojan Woman Ssssh. It is beginning.

Maira appears in her nightshirt, with a puppet show.

Maira Ten years of war. Ten years our great city besieged but not defeated. The dead litter the battlefield. We wake to another day of bloodshed, another day hemmed into our city walls. Look – the children are first up out of their beds, desperate to find the remaining scraps of food. My brother Abas and my sister Samira.

Puppet-Maira is in her nightshirt in bed. Her puppet brother and sister come to her.

Abas Sister!

Samira Sister, come and see. The Greeks are gone.

Maira Don't be silly – stop dreaming and go back to bed.

Abas Sister, I am not dreaming. Look between the cracks of the city walls made by their assaults.

Samira Listen to the silence after ten years' bombing.

Maira rises.

Maira Silence in the city. And beyond the walls – (*She rubs her eyes.*) Nothing. Gone the battalions. Gone the legions of horsemen, the tents with the Argive banners furling in the hot air. Not a sign of a Greek sword. All vanished in one night.
They've gone. They've gone!

A party.

Song
> The Greeks they are gone. Go-go-go-gone.
> Oh life will be lively and life will be fun
> Now that the Greeks are gone.
>
> The Greeks they have fled. I hope they are dead.
> The Greeks they have upped ship and disappear-ed.
> Praise God that the Greeks have gone.
>
> After ten years of hate. Let's ce-celebrate.
> Let's let down our hair and in-inebriate
> Now that the Greeks are gone.
>
> The Greeks they are gone. Go-go-go-gone.
> Oh life will be lively and life will be fun
> Now that the Greeks are gone.

Music of celebration. A puppet dance of joy. Amidst this dance of joy the wooden horse appears. It is gigantic beside the puppet Trojans. The dancing fades.

Abas What is that that stands outside our gates?

Maira A wooden horse silently stands outside the city. How did it get there? What does it mean? The people discussed.

Trojan 1 I believe that the horse is a trick. We must not bring it within our walls but hack it open with our spears with our army at the ready to kill any enemy within.

Trojan 2 I agree that treachery lies behind this strange appearance. But if we truly suspect it, we must not open it, but drag it to the cliff's edge and push it over, destroying it and any evil contained within.

Maira The people roared their approval of this opinion and the horse began to be dragged towards the cliff.

Trojans Heave! Heave!

Maira But then a third voice spoke.

Trojan 3 My friends. The Greeks have left. They have set fire to their shelters, taken up their camp and slipped away in the night like frightened rabbits. What have we to fear from them? This horse is not a threat, but a tribute from them to the gods, to safeguard their journey home. It contains great riches. They have made it too big to bring through our gate, for they know that if we can bring this horse within our city, the gods' generosity shall be aimed not on them but upon us. Let us carry it over our walls, bring it within our city and the riches shall be ours as reward for our resistance. If we throw it over the great cliff, it will all be lost. Let us haul this horse over our walls and change the course of history!

A roar of approval.

Maira No one knew who spoke. But we Trojans roared. And deep in the horse's bowels, Odysseus smiled.

Trojans Carry the horse over the walls!

Maira The catastrophic engine was heaved over. The children escorted it, singing songs and bearing palms of victory.

The horse is pulled over. She sings.

Oh my country!
Oh Ilium, home to the gods!
Oh Troy!
Four times the horse halts at the walls
Four times the sound of soldiers sounds
Four times betrayal echoes through Troy

We are deafened by madness
We do not pause
Until destruction stands in our holy place.
Oh my country!
Oh Ilium. Oh Ilium.

There we left it for one night in praise of the gods.

*Exeunt all except Odysseus. Night falls. Maira walks
forward and opens the horse. She takes out Odysseus'
puppet, in military costume.*

Puppet Odysseus Kill the sentries. Burn the houses,
block up the narrow streets so none can escape. Take the
citadel and kill the priests. Do not let the people rise up
to fight but kill them in their beds. Do not let the young
live to grow into our enemies. Kill them in their innocence.
Do not let the women see their children die lest they be
turned into furies. Kill them in their homes. Spare no
one. As my name is Odysseus, kill all!

*Greeks pour out of the wooden horse. The puppet-
Trojans are torn apart and blood pours out of the
horse. The puppets lie strewn across the stage. The
puppet Odysseus stands astride the horse surveying
the damage. Puppet Maira is running.*

Maira Curiosity saved me. I who wanted to see the horse
at night, saw instead the arrival of our killers. I ran back
to my family but the tide of Greek soldiers was too fast.
I was cut off. I ducked down narrow alleys, hid in
doorways, begged for a cloud to cover the moon. It was
dawn before I could get home.

*Puppet Maira sees puppet Abas and Samira in pieces
on the ground.*

Abas? Samira? (*Puppet Maira crumples to the ground
and weeps.*) Mother? Father? Friends? Neighbours?

Countrymen?
What has happened to us at the hands of Odysseus?

Oh my country!
Oh Ilium, home to the gods!
Oh Troy!
Our destruction stands in our holy place.
Oh my country!
Oh Ilium. Oh Ilium.

Odysseus stares at the scene with eyes of horror.
Enter Interrogator 1.

Interrogator 1 Ah, there you are. I've been looking for you. What's this, a puppet show? Very nice, good to see you keeping yourselves entertained.

I've got good news for you, sir. The boat's down at the harbour and ready to set sail. First-class treatment. Champagne. Three-course dinner courtesy of the Prime Minister himself, with our apologies for any misunderstanding that may have taken place. I just need you to confirm your name and sign this piece of paper.

Pause. Odysseus does nothing.

Interrogator 1 It's a mere formality, I can assure you. Just sign your name, confirm your identity, and we're away.

Pause.

Odysseus My name is Nobody.

Interrogator 1 I don't think so. Come on, sir, the boat's waiting. Think of your lovely wife waiting for you. It's been twenty years, I would have thought you might be in a bit of a hurry.

The Trojans are listening.

Odysseus My name is Nobody.

Interrogator 1 Listen, we can do this alone, if there are any issues. No need to make a public display of it. Let's just go.

Odysseus I am Nobody.

Interrogator 1 You are General Odysseus of Ithaca. That's not nobody. Now come on.

Odysseus I am Nobody.

Interrogator 1 Listen, if you don't sign this, you can forget the whole thing. No boat, no champagne. Nothing.

Pause.

You better not have been winding me up, mate. I have vouched for you.

Odysseus Just get out. Get out!

Interrogator 1 How dare you? I have gone out on a limb for you. There are people who think I've gone soft in the head. Sign the paper. (*He pushes the paper in Odysseus' face.*) Sign the paper. Sign the paper! (*Odysseus rips up the paper. Interrogator starts to strangle Odysseus.*) I'll kill you. I'll lock you up and throw away the key! (*He stops strangling Odysseus and stands furious but helpless. Beat.*) I should have known. Like I always tell Harold: never get too involved!

Exit Interrogator 1.

Odysseus I am Odysseus, general of the Greek army, sacker of Troy and wanderer of the seas. Do with me as you wish.

The Trojans move into action. They appear to be constructing a gibbet. A wooden pole, a wooden platform, a rope. Odysseus obediently gets up and takes the rope, places it round his neck.
Maira takes it from his neck. She uses it to hoist

a sail. The sound of the sea.

Odysseus What are you doing?

Maira You are truly lucky, Odysseus. There's a fair wind.

The boat sets sail across the sea. The Trojans sing.

Song
　　These stars are not my stars.
　　This sea is not my own.
　　This pale moon is not my moon.
　　This world is not my home.

　　This sail is not my sail.
　　This ship is not my own.
　　This pale sky is not my sky.
　　This world is not my home.

　　These eyes are not my eyes.
　　This skin is not my skin.
　　This pale sun is not my sun.
　　Till I see my home again.
　　Till I see my home again.

Ithaca. Dawn. Odysseus stands alone on the shore. The Trojans have gone. An old man stands staring at Odysseus: Eumaeus.

Odysseus What country is this?

Old Man This is Ithaca. Who are you?

The sea fades into silence.

The End.

CRIME AND PUNISHMENT IN DALSTON

with help from
Fyodor Dostoevsky and David Fishley

for the Arcola Theatre

Crime and Punishment in Dalston was first performed at the Arcola Theatre, on 3 January 2002. The cast was as follows:

Darius Dave Fishley
Raz Learie Foster
Sevgi Michelle Hallak
Campbell Andrew Melville
Brother/Shopkeeper Cengiz Bozkurt
Young Girl Inji Karagil

Director David Farr
Assistant Director Tiffany Watt-Smith
Designer Angela Simpson
Lighting Colin Grenfell
Sound Ian Dickinson
Music Artists from the Pedro Youth Club,
    Homerton Estate, Hackney
Music Co-ordinator Isa Soares

Characters

Darius
Sevgi
Raz
Campbell
Sevgi's Brother
Old Turkish Man
Granddaughter
Voice of Darius' Mother
Man
People

Act One

THE CRIME

Darius' room in an ex-council house in Dalston.
Darius alone in his room. Night. Light from the street.
Passing police cars. Passing noise. Darius sleeping on a
single mattress on the floor. Almost hidden by blankets
that cover him. It is winter and the room is without
heating but for a single-bar electric heater, which glows
red in the darkness.
The phone rings. The answerphone clicks on. Darius'
voice.

Voice of Darius There's no one here. Don't leave a
message.

A beep. The voice of Darius' mother on the
answerphone.

Voice of Mother Darius? Is this the number for Darius
Jacobs? I've been calling this number but I keep getting
no reply. Darius, is this your phone? Six months I've not
heard from you, Darius. I know you're busy. I know
you've got a lot going on in London. But couldn't you
find five minutes to talk to your own mother? God help
me, you're my boy, Darius, you're in my heart . . .

The machine clicks off. The shapeless form starts to
cough and shake on the bed. It crawls across the floor
to the fridge. Opens it and takes out drink. Sits in the
fridge-door light.

Darius What are people most afraid of? Of saying
something new, a new word of their own that hasn't been

said before – that's what scares them. Doing something that has never been done.

Blackout.

A tape is playing. Darius is doing exercises. Faster and faster. Blackout.

Day. Darius, feverish. Sitting with a letter at the table.

Darius They've upped the rent. How can they do that? Half the lights don't work, there's water running down the walls, and they've upped the rent. Didn't even come and talk to me about it. Sent me a letter. Well, they can take their letter and . . . I'll leave. I've got places to go. I've got options. I don't have to sit back and take this.

He stands behind the counter, just like any old Turkish man selling cabbages. Doesn't even smile. Just stares at me like I'm a criminal. I want to say, you're the fucking criminal! You're the one with the rent racket! So don't fucking stare at me!

Here's how it works. He gets each of his family to move into a council house. Few months later they buy the house cheap off the council. Now they have five houses to rent out. Then they change their name and buy another five. Pretty soon they've got over twenty houses. He rents them, a room at a time, to the likes of me. Stupid black suckers who are happy to live in shit while he makes a fucking fortune.

They say he doesn't trust banks. They say he keeps his money in the back of the shop. They say.

I'm rambling. That's why I never do anything – I'm too busy rambling. That's why no black man ever does anything – we're too busy talking about it. How long have I been lying here in my thoughts, whole days and nights in this room? This fucking room. This heat burning inside me. Furnace in my head. Should go out. Get some air. Get some air.

He does not move. Blackout.

Lights up. The flat. Darius looking out of the window.

We owned these roads once. Our streets. We were given them like the dirtiest dog gets the dirtiest corner of the yard. And what did we do? We made it dirtier. We lay in our own shit, scratched our balls and laughed. Then the Turks came. They took our leaking shops and made them work. They took our houses and made them theirs. In ten years they turned Hackney into fucking Istanbul. And we let them do it. We let them take it and now we're too busy licking our wounds, and buying our green off of them to do nothing about it. They control us like they control the heroin and the booze and the gambling. We're just a cog in their business operation.

Look outside – the names are in a language that is not my language, the food is not my food, the gambling clubs are not open to me. And they keep us like that so we don't even get near the white man. The Turk is the white man's prison guard. And if you want to break out of prison, you don't have to kill the governor. You just have to kill the guard.

Blackout.

Lights up. Darius comes through the door.

Darius Just been to the rehearsal. I went late when he's normally alone – just before closing.

  The old Turkish man appears. Darius holds out a bracelet.

Darius I've come about the rent . . . I know I'm late. I'm late because I haven't got it. I had to spend the benefit on something else. Like food. No, wait. Listen to me! I've got an offer. I'll give you this. It's pure silver. My mother gave it me. It must be worth a hundred at least. (*He keeps the bracelet at arm's length from the shopkeeper.*) But I want you to know something. I'm coming back for it. I'll come back and I'll take what's mine.

  Blackout.

Lights up. A black man stands, whip in hand. Darius is dreaming.

Darius Jamaica. Middle of the day. Middle of fucking nowhere. You're a boy. You're with your dad waiting for a bus back into town. Sun blistering down. A man stands outside a bar. Drunk on bad rum. He has a cart pulled by an old grey mare. A worthless old nag.

Man Come on! I'm taking you all back up the hill on my buggy!

Darius Voices from the bar. What you doing, man? Harnessing that old filly to that great cart? She'll never pull it!

Man Just get in, man! I'm telling you – she'll make it. I'll make she make it! I feel like doing her in anyway – all she does is eat my oats and give nothing back!

People That mare hasn't galloped in ten years!

Man Well, she's gon' gallop now!

Darius They're climbing onto the cart. Must be twenty of them. They're shouting, singing, holding guitars and sticks, some high on weed, some drunk on rum. What are they doing? Papa, what are they doing?

Man (*cracking the whip*) Giddy-up!

People We're not going nowhere, man. She's too weak. Look 'pon her knees!

Man Yes we are! Just watch her go, boys!

Darius She doesn't move. She can't move!

Man I'll flog her to death if it comes to that!

He is flogging wildly. The wild noise of a horse in agony.

People Whip her on the muzzle, on the eyes! On the eyes!

Darius No stop! Stop!

People He's going to kill her! / He's going to do her in!

Man She belongs to me! (*He is beating her with all his might.*)

People Take an iron to her! Get it over with! / Do her in! Do her in!

Man Give me that iron! Watch out!

Darius Papa, stop him!

People Kill her! Kill her!

Man She belongs to me!

Darius Stop!

Man She belongs to me!

He lifts the crowbar and brings it down on the horse's head. Darius screams and wakes.

Darius Oh God. Will I really do it? Will I really take an axe and hit him on the head with it, smash his skull in? Will I slip on his warm sticky blood, break open the till, steal the money and tremble; then hide myself, covered in blood . . . with the axe . . . will I really?

What's got into me? I knew I didn't have the stamina for this. Why have I been torturing myself all this time? Even when I went to do that rehearsal . . . I knew I'd never be able to go through with it . . . Sick! No, I couldn't. I couldn't go through with it. Not even if there were no uncertainties. Not even if I was sure. I couldn't go through with it, I couldn't, and that's it! So why, why, even now . . .

Blackout.

Lights up. Darius brings out an axe from a pile of clothes. He ties it into the loop of his coat. He is sweating. He moves towards the door, then stops, seeing his face in the television.

Darius I look pale. He'll be suspicious. Should I wait until later? But if I wait the shop might close, and the best time is just before closing when there is no one around. But shouldn't I at least wait here until my heart has quietened down? Yes, I should wait. I should wait.

I'll wait. (*At which point he puts on coat and cap and leaves abruptly.*)

The shop of the Old Turkish Man. It is being redecorated. The shopkeeper closes the shutter halfway down for the night. He sits behind the counter and counts his money.
   Enter Darius in the doorway, under the shutter, cap over his head, thick coat. Pause.

Darius All right?

   Pause.

I've . . . brought you something . . . can I come inside?

Old Shopkeeper We are closing.

Darius This won't take long. (*He enters.*) You're redecorating. It looks nice.

Old Shopkeeper What do you want? What's your business?

Darius Don't you recognise me? I'm one of your tenants. I came three days ago with the bracelet. Don't you remember?

   Pause.

Old Shopkeeper You have the money?

Darius No, I have something else. My last thing. The last thing in the world. I have it for you. (*Pause.*) What are you staring at me like that for? If you want it, take it, and if you don't want it, I'll go to someone else and sell it and bring you your money. I don't have time for this, man.

Old Shopkeeper There's no need to get angry.

Darius There's no need to look suspicious.

Old Shopkeeper Show me.

He holds out a small wrapped package, his hand shaking. The man takes it.

You're sick?

Darius What?

Old Shopkeeper You. Sick.

Darius Yes. Fever. Haven't had nothing to eat.

Old Shopkeeper You should go to bed.

Darius Why don't you take a look?

The man starts to open the package. It is difficult and he turns to a light to see what he is doing. Darius reaches inside his coat.

Old Shopkeeper Why have you wrapped it so tight?

He opens it and finds a block of wood. Darius freezes for a second, then takes the axe out, and with sudden speed he brings the axe down on the old man's head. He crumples and he hits him again, and then again. He lies dead on the floor of the shop. Darius puts the axe down next to him, and reaches inside the man's pocket for his keys, finds them, then runs to the till. He opens it and grabs the money. He suddenly sits on the floor. Then just as suddenly rises again, runs back to the body to check he is still dead. He is. He feels something in the man's clothes, and finds a purse. Inside the purse is a key. Then he runs to the back of the shop and finds a chest. He opens the chest with the key. He starts to rub his hands on the red lining.

Darius It's red so it won't show so much. (*Beat.*) I didn't bring a bag. Christ! What was I thinking of?

He ransacks the place to find a sack, then starts to fill it with some money. Then he stops dead.

A figure appears through the door under the shutter. A figure of a fourteen-year-old girl enters the shop. Darius freezes. A pause.

Girl (*in Turkish*) Grandad? Grandad where are you?

She approaches the body, and is about to scream. Darius doesn't stop to think, but dashes out to her, takes the axe, and lands a blow directly on her skull. She falls like dead weight to the floor.

He stops for a moment, then dashes to the door in the shutter and bolts it.

Darius How could I forget to lock it? How could I?

Pause. He looks at the body. He runs to fetch the money and the axe. He suddenly opens the door in the shutter. No one is there. He flies out into the night, shutting the door behind him.

Act Two

SEVGI

Night. Darius in bed. The sounds of people passing in the night, drunk.

Darius Ah, that'll be the brothers back from the clubs. I wonder if they pulled tonight. Some will be high. I'd like to get high. What time is it? Maybe I could go out. To a club. I wonder what time it is. (*He turns on the TV.*) Gone two. Is that too late? Nah, there'll be a club still open somewhere.

> *He turns to see the axe lying on the table where he must have dropped it amidst his clothes and the sack. He enters a total panic. He starts to undress, to check every piece of clothing for blood.*

No blood. No blood. Yes! You're a fuckin' pro! The money. The sack. Hide it. Hide it!

> *He takes the sack and hides it behind a rack of clothes. Then stops dead.*

Christ! You call that hidden! Are those things even like remotely hidden! (*Laughs.*) Why am I laughing? I'm losing it, man. I'm losing the plot, man! Ha ha ha.

> *He starts to shiver uncontrollably. He faints. Sudden blackout. Equally sudden lights up. He wakes.*

How could I fall asleep when nothing's been done? Think. I haven't done nothing. I haven't even torn out that loop!

> *He tears out the loop from his coat and stuffs it in a pillow on his bed. Then he stops dead.*

Blood. There is blood. How could I not see it? Anyone coming in could have seen it. And there's blood on my trousers. Ha. Ha! This is it, is it? Is my punishment already beginning? Yes. Yes. I knew it! And there was blood on the purse. I remember. Blood on the purse. Yes. Here it is. That means there'll be blood in the pocket. Yes there is. That's cool, man. That means my reason is still working, I worked it out, I'm still sound, man. I'm sound. But now what do I do? Do I cut it off? Yes. Cut it off.

He fetches some scissors and snips at the trousers, cutting off the bloodied ends and the pocket.

No! Hide them! Would they burn? But what with? No, I should take them outside and throw them away. Yes, that's what I should do. (*He sits down.*) I must throw them away without delay! Yes, without delay! Come on! You must take the stuff right now! Take it right now and throw it away! Get it out of sight quickly! Quickly! Quickly!

He lies down. Blackout.

Light up. Darius wakes.

Darius What time is it?

He sees the TV, turns up the volume.

Newscaster And now, with the time approaching seven o'clock, the news . . .

He turns off the news. Runs to pull on some trousers.

Darius What am I doing? What am I doing? I haven't hidden anything! OK. OK. Let's go. (*Then, in dressing,*

93

he sees marks on his shoes.) Blood on my shoes. On my
socks. How could I not see that? OK, wash them and
then go. Wash and go. (*Sings.*) 'Wash and Go!' Ha ha ha.

*He takes the shoes and washes them. There is a knock
at his door. He freezes.*

Voice of Raz Hey, D-man, you sleeping? Let us in, man.
Darius, man, it's Raz, I need a piss, man. Hey, D-man –
it's just me – Raz. Remember me? We was friends before
you turned into some kind of fucked-up hermit freako.

*Darius, in an insane panic, runs across the room
fetching axe, sack and bits of trouser and putting
them in a sports bag along with the shoes.*

Listen, you want me to piss on your door? Christ, it's
not like you're working in the morning. 'Cos you ain't
ever worked and I know it.

*Darius stuffs the bag under a table and turns to
survey the room.*

I swear to you, man, you don't let me in, I am going to
break this door down. I am a man in dire need of a piss.

*He starts to beat at the door. Darius opens the door
but bars it.*

Ah, the man himself. Well you gonna let me in or am
I gonna piss on your feet?

*Darius lets him in. Raz runs to the bathroom, pisses,
then comes back and stops in shock.*

Raz Christ. What has happened to this place? Something
says to me you haven't been going out much recently,
brother.

*He tries to turn on the main light, but it does not
work.*

Darius Bulb's gone.

Raz You can buy others just like it, did you know that?

Darius opens the curtains. Grey dawn daylight creeps into the room. Raz sees Darius.

Raz Well, fuck me. What has happened to you? You look like a dead man.

Darius Nothing.

Raz Fuck nothing. Let me feel your head. You got a fever, brother.

Darius I'm fine.

Raz You need to see a doctor.

Darius No doctors! I just need to eat something. I've had this temperature but it's going.

Raz It won't go nowhere until you heat this ice cube up.

Darius Gas is cut off.

Raz Jesus.

Darius Why are you here?

Raz Well, I was on my way home after satisfying a certain young lady who possesses the proverbial hunger of the wolf, and who happens to live in the very same area as my old friend Mr D. It's been a long time, man. I left messages. I even came round once but no reply. Hey. Have you shifted any of those CDs I gave you?

Pause.

The CDs I gave you to sell down the market? You said you were going to start a stall. I left them behind your door.

Pause. They are still behind the door.

95

Fuck you, bro, I needed you to sell some of those CDs.
I have ambitions in the music industry, did you know
that? I can't afford for my talent to be lying behind your
fucking door.

Darius I got busy.

Raz Yeah right, staring at your navel, you were very
fucking busy.

Darius Take them back. They're no use to me now.

Pause. Footsteps outside. Darius freezes.

It's them.

Raz It's who?

Darius It's them. Well, let them come. Let it be over
once and for all.

*The footsteps stop outside Darius' door and a letter is
pushed under the door. Raz goes to pick it up and
hands it to Darius. Darius opens it and reads.*

Voice of Mother Dear Son, I don't even know if you
will get this or if I'm just throwing money into the wind.
I love you, son, I cry at night thinking about you. If you
get this, buy something nice for yourself. It's a beautiful
life God gave us, Darius, and he only gave us one.
God bless you. Your mother.

*Inside is one hundred pounds in cash. Darius holds it,
and is overwhelmed by shaking. Feet, teeth, his whole
body in a spasm. Raz tries to hold him but is unable
as Darius collapses to the floor.*

Blackout.

Lights up. Darius is sleeping. Raz enters with two plastic bags full of stuff. He tidies the room a little, puts in a new bulb. He sees the sports bag and is curious about something sticking out from it, when Darius awakes.

Darius What you doing?

Raz Just trying to get this place into some order.

Darius What are you doing here?

Raz What am I doing? I'm taking care of you, you fucking crazy. So, you've finally woken from the coma.

Darius How long have I been sleeping?

Raz You've been drifting in and out for four days.

Darius Four days?

Raz You were a man in bad need of a snooze.

Darius Did I say anything? In my sleep – did I say anything?

Raz You said some weird shit, man.

Darius What did I say? What did I say!

Raz Hey, get off me, man! Don't fucking touch me like that!

Darius What did I say?

Raz What gratitude is that? I look after you, I get a doctor in to see you, and that's my reward! I'm not your fucking mother.

Darius A doctor has been here?

Raz Twice. First time he was worried you might be about to wave goodbye to us all, but he's well happy now.

Darius I told you no doctors! I told you!

Raz Well, you weren't in much of a state to discuss it.

Darius What did I say?

Raz Relax, man. You didn't say nothing about women or green. You spoke mainly about your socks. You kept saying, 'Give me my socks, I want my socks.' Fucking cracked me up, man. And then you asked for the ends of your trousers, you got all emotional about them, man. I'm thinking there must be something real special about the ends of them trousers. And this got me thinking about you and your clothes and your conditions, man. So what do you think I've been doing while you slept? Well, since you ask I'll tell you. I took some of the money your sweet mama sent you and I've been down Ridley Road. For who was it said that the clothes make the man? (*He reaches into his bag.*) Let's start at the top and work down. Item! One nearly new blue cap with obligatory white Nike tick, authenticity guaranteed, a bargain at £4.99. Item! One absolute bona fide Tommy Hilfiger T-shirt, £24.99 in any West End shop, to you, seven pounds. Item! One jacket, five pounds second hand, would have been fifty new, minimum. Item! One pair of bottoms, simple black because we don't want cheap showy trash, no sir, we are not from the Elephant and Castle, and then finally – and this I am really proud of – Item! One pair of Nike Classic creps! Now I couldn't find your shoes to take with me – I'm wondering if you actually have some? – so I took a measurement of your sleeping feet and I reckon these will fit just fine. A bit beat-up yes, but seeing as you don't have £89.99 to spend right now, I offer these as a perfect blend of style and integrity. So lay it on me big, man, what do you think? Pretty good for sixty quid, and still leaving you forty to acquire food, drink, and of course, shades, which I did not presume to buy seeing as they are deeply a matter of the personal palette.

Darius I don't want all this.

Raz Well, you're having it, bro, 'cos I ain't taking up a whole lot of my valuable time for nothing. I'm a businessman with a finger in many pies, I can't afford to be leaving my interests to lie fallow while I look after my fucked-up friends. But to show that I am not bitter, and to give you an opportunity to present the new image of Darius Jacobs to the world, I am inviting you to an exclusive check-it-out strictly-invitation-only party tonight. There'll be bare heads there, bro, and you had better be making an appearance.

Darius I can't come.

Raz I mean, your diary is just crammed full of engagements brother.

Darius I won't come!

Raz D, there'll be enough buff tings for you to feast your eyes on for a year!

Darius I won't come to your party! Can't you get it into your skull that I don't want to? This good-deed bullshit. Tell me, man, what can I do to get you off my back? I'm willing to admit that I'm mean and ungrateful, if you'll just fuck off and leave me alone!

Pause.

Raz Suit yourself, brother. Suit yourself.

Darius It will all be over soon, anyway.

Raz What will?

Darius You'll see. Just go.

Raz I hear you. Loud and clear. (*He opens to leave.*) Oh, by the way. You heard about the Turkish shopkeeper on Kingsland Road?

Darius What about him?

Raz Nothing's about him right now. Axed to death along with his granddaughter. Some fucked-up crackhead. That by way of showing you there are people in this world worse off than you. People with metal blades in their skulls. You know where to find me.

Exit Raz. Darius grabs the clothes and starts to dress.

Darius I must lose the stuff. It was there all this time. Four days! He could have looked in it at any moment! I should just go to the station right now, go down on my knees and confess everything. Then it would be over! No! That's what they want! They want weakness! They want surrender! Hide the bag. Yes! Throw it away and it will all be over! But where? Maybe the canal? But people will see me. No! No! I must take it far away! The Thames! But they always find things in the Thames. That kid's torso, they found that. Where then? I must do it now! Oh where? Where?

Blackout.

Lights up. Sports-hall changing room. Darius enters with sports sack. Men are showering behind and talking as Darius opens the locker and deposits the bag. A white man is speaking.

Man They were found by the grandson in the morning. There was blood in the vegetables and everything. It was like a fucking red sea . . . They reckon he had getting on for five hundred quid on him. Those fucking heroin addicts would kill their own grandmothers for five hundred. You know I heard this black guy on the street say, 'If I met the man who did it, I'd shake his fucking hand.' You know what I'd do? I'd cut it off.

On the street.

Darius I never counted the money. Christ, man, if you really were fucking sound about this, then how is it you didn't count to see how much was inside? What was that about?

I just want this over with! Yes. Today must be the day. This must be brought to an end today! Because I don't want to go on living like this!

A bar. Darius reads the old newspapers and finds the article.

Darius Here it is. Front page. 'Detective Inspector Bishop condemned this brutal and cowardly crime.' Brutal and cowardly. Who makes up these words, man? Do lots of policemen sit in meetings figuring out the most suitable words for every fucking crime? No wonder they don't ever solve nothing. (*Reads.*) 'A black youth was seen running from the area.' Ha ha ha. There. It's beginning.

> *Unseen by Darius, a Turkish girl has sat down near him: Sevgi. She has a vodka and is smoking. He has not noticed her.*

It's beginning. Not long now before they find more evidence, fingerprints, and they'll come after me. No,

it will be over soon. It will all be over. (*He sees her.*)
Were you listening? Were you listening? (*He is half-strangling her.*)

Sevgi To what?

Darius To what I was saying.

Sevgi You didn't say nothing. You have been sitting there staring at the newspaper for twenty minutes.

Darius Is that a crime?

Sevgi No.

Darius Then stop looking at me!

   Pause.

Do you want to know what I was looking at?

Sevgi No.

Darius This.

Sevgi . . .

Darius What do you think of a person who did something like that?

Sevgi I don't want to talk about it.

Darius Why not? I mean what else is there to talk about?

Sevgi My sister knew the girl. She came to our house. They did ballet dancing together.

Darius Was she a good dancer?

Sevgi How should I know? Anyway, what does it matter?

Darius Yes, what does it matter? She's dead.

Sevgi Yes. She's dead.

Darius But why would someone do that?

Sevgi Drugs, I suppose.

Darius Why do you think it was drugs?

Sevgi What else?

Darius But how can you be sure?

Sevgi They took her money . . .

Darius Lots of people need money.

Sevgi But they don't kill to get it.

Darius Do you think they'll catch him?

Sevgi How should I know?

Darius They saw a black man running away.

Sevgi So?

Darius So you're Turkish, aren't you . . .?

Sevgi So what?

Darius Aren't you angry? A black man kills a defenceless old man and his granddaughter. A black man like me. Doesn't that make you angry?

Sevgi Yes, it does.

Darius So you're angry with me as a representative of the black race?

Sevgi No.

Darius Is that why you're talking to me? To try to deal with that anger you feel? To remind yourself that not all black men are like that bastard that did that?

Sevgi No!

Darius So why are you talking to me? I could know the man that did that. I could know him well.

Sevgi You don't.

Darius But I could.

Sevgi Fuck you. Fuck you! I didn't ask to talk to you. I was just sitting here getting myself drunk, I didn't want no conversation! OK?

Darius Where are you going?

Sevgi To find somewhere where I can drink without being hassled. (*She starts to leave the bar.*)

Darius No wait. Wait! I'm sorry. Please. Let me buy you a drink, and then I'll go.

Sevgi You want to buy me a drink?

Darius Yeah.

Sevgi And then you'll leave?

Darius Yeah.

Pause.

Sevgi I want a double vodka and tonic.

Darius Double vodka and tonic!

Pause.

I'm going.

Sevgi You don't want a drink?

Dorian I've been ill. I shouldn't. I shouldn't.

Sevgi Suit yourself.

Pause.

Darius I'll have a coffee. (*He sits.*) You don't normally come here.

Sevgi You must be joking. I ain't allowed to come to places like this.

Darius Why are you here now?

Sevgi I just needed to get away.

Darius From what?

Sevgi Everything. I want another.

Darius Let me.

Sevgi It's OK.

Darius No, let me! I want to, I made a heap of money recently, honest. I'm flush, man.

Sevgi OK.

   Pause. The vodka arrives and she downs it in one.

Don't fancy getting us another, do you?

Darius Is there something wrong?

Sevgi There's a whole bunch.

Darius Do you want to tell me?

Sevgi How long have you got?

Darius I've got a long time.

   Pause.

Sevgi My father has no job. Mum works in the factory, my brothers do bits and pieces, but he can't find nothing. He has this idea to start an off-licence in my area. We have some family savings. Ten grand or thereabouts. He needs ten grand more. Mum says wait a while, we'll raise the money. But my dad's always in a hurry. Yesterday he goes to the coffee shop. He starts to gamble. But the numbers aren't high enough. He's only winning fifty quid here, losing it there. He hears about this place up in Haringey. He goes there at midnight. He's with a cousin. By two he has won another five thousand. He buys some beers to celebrate. He goes back and plays some more. There are some faces he doesn't recognise. But he's feeling lucky. He loses the five. Then another five. He loses the lot. The cousin says come home. He won't. He goes back to the table. He stakes the house. I get back tonight and there are men in our kitchen. Dad's disappeared. They want us out by tomorrow morning, unless we can pay rent on the house. Mum says I have to stop college and go to work. Go into the factory like her. I say no way. I've got exams in six months. I'm not working in no factory. We fight. I leave.

Pause.

I will drink myself to death but I ain't working in no factory.

Darius Take this.

Sevgi What is it?

Darius Tell your mum that's for starters.

Sevgi I can't take it. She'll think I'm dealing or something.

Darius Tell her you sold some clothes. But tell her you must stay in college. I'll have more for you soon.

Sevgi I can't accept.

Darius You have no choice! You have to do things you don't want when you have no choice! I am a stranger and you must rely on me. I have lots of money, I've been very lucky, I can spare more, but I can't get my hands on it yet. You understand? I mean, this is what it was all for! Yes! This is what it was for!

Sevgi What was?

Darius Meet me here tomorrow! I'll bring you more. Yes! This is what it is for!

Sevgi Where are you going?

Darius What's your name?

Sevgi Sevgi.

Darius Sevgi. Go home. Tell your mum there'll be more tomorrow. There'll be more tomorrow!

Darius alone on the street.

Darius Be gone, mirages! Be gone, affected terrors. Be gone, apparitions! There's a life to be lived! Now is the kingdom of reason and light! Freedom and strength! And now we shall see! Now we shall measure swords! I will live. I will live!

Raz's party. Raz is drunk and high and happy. Darius enters.

Raz I knew he'd come! Didn't I just say it? He said he wouldn't but I knew he would! I knew he couldn't resist the prospect of fucking some of the most beautiful pussy in North London. And look at him. A vision! A fucking catwalk vision of cool!

Darius I just came to say that I'm sorry for what I said and that maybe there is hope for all men.

Raz Pass that by me again, man.

Darius The truth is that no one can tell what may happen to him.

Raz That's cool, man, I mean I didn't actually understand a single fucking word that you said, but that's cool. You want some green? It's quality shit, man. Hey, man, let me introduce you to . . . come here, man, come here, I have a lady through there who desires to meet your acquaintance. I mean, I have given you such a fucking build-up, man, you will have to puke on her not to score.

Darius I can't join you.

Raz Man, she is creaming herself for you, baby . . . where you going?

Darius I'm going home.

Raz Man, you only just got here!

Darius stumbles.

Hey, steady there.

Darius I'm OK. Really I am. But come tomorrow. Will you?

Raz Wait! D-man, wait. (*Pause.*) I'll walk you home.

Darius What about the party?

Raz Hmmn? Oh. Fuck that piece of shit. All the buff girls have gone home. The decent green ran out an hour ago. For the last forty minutes this so-called party has comprised twenty black men sitting round offering us the riches of their minds. Well, you know what, and I don't care who hears this, I am bored of listening to the black man moan. Moan about money, moan about not getting enough pussy, moan about getting too much pussy, moan about the sky being blue, moan about rain being wet,

I swear to you put a black man in paradise he'll moan about the curtains. (*to the room*) You hearing me, brothers? Yes, I said that. You want to come outside and talk about it! You want to?

Darius I can make it home alone.

Raz You know what these pussy-hos have been chatting about in here for the last hour? They've been chatting bare shit about the 'media representation' of the murder of the Turkish shopkeeper. They are saying that the papers have misrepresented the case, that they have blown the thing up into an atrocity. Hello? An axe is taken to two innocent people in their own shop and we're the victims! (*to the room*) What am I saying? I'm saying maybe we should take a good look at ourselves. I'm saying whoever did that was an evil fucked-up little son of a bitch and he's no brother of mine. But you know what that opinion makes me in this room? That makes me a Judas. That makes me a member of the Ku Klux fucking Klan.

(*to the room*) Yes, I said that! You got a problem with that? You want beef? Come on then, I'll take you! I'll take all of you! (*to Darius*) Run.

A street. Raz and Darius. 3 a.m. Police cars flying by.

Raz Have we lost them?

Darius I think so.

Raz Some people have no sense of humour. So what's up, blood? You've got a kind of sheen on you, like someone's been polishing you.

Darius Oh nothing. Well, actually, I think I just met an angel, only she's not an angel of course, but her coat did kind of have wings, and I gave her all my money, all of it, and it was so good, man, as if I was kissed by an angel. But actually I'm chatting bare shit, I'm so weak, could you help me . . .

Raz What's the matter with you?

Darius My head's kind of going round, but that's not what it is. It's that I feel so sad. So sad. Like a woman.

Raz Bro, am I glad you didn't say that in the party. Let's get you home, brother. Let's get you home.

In Darius' room. Raz helping him in. Laying him down on the bed. He turns on a corner light. He sees the answerphone blinking.

Raz You got a message, bro.

He presses play. A man's voice. Campbell's.

Voice of Campbell This is a message for Mr Darius Jacobs. Would you please come to Stoke Newington police station tomorrow at ten o'clock and ask for Mr Campbell. Thank you.

Blackout.

Act Three

CAMPBELL

A police interview room. Darius and Raz.

Raz I don't know what this is about, but you just say
nothing, man.
   You keep quiet, they don't have nothing on you.
   You keep it zipped, know what I mean?
   Say nothing, you hear me?

   Enter Campbell. Raz puts on shades.

Campbell Which of you gentlemen is . . .

Darius I'm the one you want.

Campbell Mr Jacobs. And you are . . .

Raz I'm a friend.

Campbell Well, that's very nice of you. But I think you
may be wasting your time.

Raz I'll decide that.

Campbell As you wish. Mr Jacobs, we need you to sign
this.

Raz Don't sign it. Don't fucking sign anything.

Campbell If you would hold on just a second . . .

Raz We want a lawyer.

Campbell That really isn't necessary.

Raz I'll decide what is necessary. Are you arresting him?

Campbell Not to my knowledge. Should we be?

Raz Well then, he's not signing nothing. Nothing, you hear me? You motherfuckers have fucked us around for too long. Now one call on my Nokia, I can get the biggest human-rights lawyer on the North East side. We know our rights, mister.

Campbell Call me Campbell.

Raz Whatever.

Campbell Are you in agreement with your friend?

Raz Yes, he is.

Campbell Well then it would seem that's all we have to discuss.

Raz See, man, they had nothing on you, they're just trying to pin some shit on you to increase their percentages. We're out of here.

Campbell So I'll give it to the charity fund, shall I?

Pause.

Darius Give what?

Campbell The bracelet. I'm assuming you don't want it back.

Raz What bracelet?

Campbell Oh, you didn't know? Mr Jacobs had a bracelet in hock with the shopkeeper who was killed. In lieu of rent, I imagine. I've been tracking all the tenants down and he's one of the last to come forward.

Pause.

Raz You were his tenant?

Campbell Oh, you didn't know. Oh, I see.

Darius That's sweet, man.

Campbell Sorry, I don't understand.

Darius You could have brought the bracelet in for me to see. That way there would have been no confusion. But this way you find out much more. That's sweet.

Campbell I assure you that what I am conducting is a staggeringly tedious logistical procedure that has taken me the best part of a week. That's the reward you get for nearing retirement. I'll be pushing the tea trolley next.

Darius Aren't you going to ask me?

Campbell Ask you to sign? I thought . . .

Darius Oh, I'll sign all right. But aren't you going to ask me . . . where I was?

Campbell When?

Darius So sweet! On the night? On that night?

Campbell Oh, I see. To be honest I had no such intention. I'm not even technically on the murder case. They really don't know what to do with me. Of course, they did say that if I should notice anything strange . . .

Darius Yes?

Campbell Listen, son.

Darius I'm not your son.

Campbell You know as well as me that this was the action of some deranged addict. There are plenty to choose from and I'm sure we'll find him. But you're not one of them. You're not even on our records.

Raz I am. You did me for thieving once. Kept me locked in this shithole for two nights. For taking a fucking bagel! So maybe you think it was me that did it? I mean I'm black, I'm available . . .

Campbell What's eating you?

Raz Nothing.

Campbell You really didn't know he was his tenant?

Raz What he tells me is his business.

Campbell But as his friend . . .

Raz I'm not his friend.

Campbell You said you were.

Raz I didn't say jack-shit!

Darius That's down to me. I've been ill – I forgot to mention it to him. Let me sign this thing and we'll be out of here. (*He does so. He stands.*)

Campbell I knew a fellow looked like you.

Beat.

It was a good few years ago now. A young man spoke at a Louis Farrakhan bash, before the ban. Caused a bit of a furore, I remember, at the time.

Pause.

Darius That was me.

Campbell I wasn't sure.

Darius You were very sure. You knew before I got here.

Campbell I can assure you that is far from being the case. Are you still involved with the Nation of Islam?

Darius I left that movement.

Campbell Why was that?

Darius I just didn't look good in a dickie-bow.

Campbell I'm trying to remember your speech. You were talking about morality.

And we are there – the young Darius is in full flow, speaking to a meeting with a mike in his hand.

Darius Morality! By morality what do we mean but the will of the white majority? By law what do we mean but the protection of the white interest? And by crime? What is a crime against the white morality, against the white law? Is it a crime at all? How many of you brothers have encountered the so-called justice of the policing system and found nothing but corruption? How many have claimed your right to a so-called fair trial and found nothing but prejudice? How then do we fight against justice? How then do we leap the system and stake our claim to a new morality – a black morality? We have to make our own path. The only place in the sun we will ever find will be one we make ourselves, in opposition to the prevailing morality, through crime, through resistance, through outrage! Do we have a right? Yes, we do! Do we have the means? Yes, we have! But this is not a journey for all men. Those that make this journey are pioneers pushing into uncharted waters. Yes, the few must lead and the many follow, for that is the lesson of history!

Campbell And who gets to choose this few?

Darius They know who they are.

Campbell How do they know?

Darius They look inside and they see.

Campbell And would you include yourself in this few?

Raz I think we should go, D-man.

Darius I wouldn't rule it out.

Raz I think we should split, man.

Darius Shut it.

Campbell So if that is the case, it would make sense to me, and please correct me if I misunderstood, that if a pioneer such as you mentioned wanted to act for the interests of black people everywhere, he should feel no compunction about doing so.

Darius Maybe so.

Campbell And if that action had dire consequences for another party, then the pioneer should understand that as a necessary sacrifice.

Darius My television tells me that collateral damage is inevitable.

Campbell The killing of a Turkish shopkeeper, for example?

Darius You said it.

Campbell And you, as one such pioneer . . .

Darius Well, if I had done that, I would surely tell you, man.

Raz Now you listen to me. This is not a legitimate investigation. You have no right to hold us here.

Campbell But my dear young friend, we are just chatting. It is the considered opinion of the station that this is a drug-related offence, and our investigations are proceeding accordingly.

Raz So why the fuck can't we go?

Campbell You can, and were always free to do so. Oh, one last thing. When did you last see the victim?

Darius Three days before he died. I took the bracelet in, as I am sure his records will show.

Campbell Notice anything strange? Apart from the redecoration.

Pause.

Darius They weren't redecorating.

Campbell Oh no, of course, no, they hadn't started then. My mistake. Well, thank you, gentlemen, I'll process this, do call in tomorrow and you can pick it up. Shall we say eleven?

The street.

Raz I don't believe that! I do not believe it! He was trying to pin that on you! That question about the decorators! If you'd not been careful, you might have made an innocent mistake and they'd have used that against you!

Darius But I was careful.

Raz Fuck them! How do they even know it was a black man? So they saw someone running away from the scene? Big deal! How do we know that's true, anyway? How do we know they didn't just cook that up so they could plant the whole thing on some unsuspecting kid who happened to be in the area? And then they have a go at you, just because you're poor, and you're sick, and you happen to have a few ideas in your head, which as we know is a crime in a black man! We should have laughed in his face, man. Or better. We should have spat in his ugly fucking mug, taken a good gobbet of spit and let fly a fucking volley of it right in his ugly racist boat.

Darius But if I had killed him, it might just have worked. I might have nodded my head just for that split second and that was all he would need.

Raz Yeah, well, he's wasting his time, because you didn't do nothing.

Darius But I could have.

Raz What do you mean?

Darius You don't know what I could have done.

Raz What you saying, man?

Darius I'm saying don't be so sure of something when you don't know nothing.

Raz Don't fuck me around, man. I saw you that night, you had a fever like a forest fire, you couldn't stand up, you weren't killing no one . . . what the fuck you doing even getting me thinking like this?

Darius laughs. Raz laughs. Darius stops laughing.

What does that mean?

Darius I'll see you later, man.

Raz Where you going?

Darius What does it matter to you?

Raz No, wait. I'm coming with you.

Darius Why won't you listen to me? I don't want you near me. Don't come to see me. Don't call me. Abandon me.

Raz What the fuck . . .

Darius Abandon me!

Pause.

Now do you understand? Do you? Do you? Now get out of here. Get out!

Lights up. Darius enters his room.

I'm a rat! A rat! If only because I am now arguing that I'm a rat, and because I conned myself that I was doing all this for a higher aim, for the good of my race, when in actual fact it was all for me myself! And because I chose such an absolute rat to squash, and finally because, because, I knew that I'd tell myself this only after I'd squashed it! Now I understand why we must be controlled like rats in a cage. That's all we are!

And the girl . . . That poor girl . . . Why did she have to turn up there like she did? It's strange, why do I hardly even think about her? As if I'd never killed her. Ballet. She did ballet.

The phone rings. Darius recoils away from it.

Voice of Darius There's no one here. Don't leave a message.

Pause.

Voice of Mother Darius? Darius are you there? Did you get my letter? Please call me or write me letting me know . . .

Darius grabs the phone.

Darius Mum, listen. No, listen to me. Listen! You are not to call me again. Don't try to find me. Just forget about me. If you love me say goodbye to me, otherwise I shall start to hate you both. I can feel it . . . I will hate you! . . . There is no fucking Lord!

He puts the phone down. Blackout.

Lights up. Darius is sleeping. A voice speaks.

Voice Murderer.

> *Pause.*

You are a murderer.

> *Darius sits up in bed.*

Darius How do you know?

Voice I saw you. I saw in your heart. I saw the evil that lies there.

Darius Can you hear me?

Voice Of course. I can hear all of your thoughts.

Darius Who are you?

Voice I'm the answering machine. I hear everything. All your thoughts and feelings. Do you want to hear some?

> *The sound of a tape rewinding. Then we hear Darius' voice.*

Voice of Darius Oh God. Will I really do it? Will I really take an axe and hit him on the head with it, smash his skull in? Will I slip on his warm sticky blood, break open the lock, steal the money and tremble; then hide myself, covered in blood . . . with the axe . . . will I really?

> *Darius reaches for the machine and presses buttons to stop the thoughts which keep replaying. He picks up the machine and screams at it.*

Darius Shut up! Shut the fuck up!

> *But now the voice comes not from the machine but from the television, which has magically switched on.*

Television Murderer! Murderer!

Darius rushes at the television, then turns to see the Shopkeeper staring at him. He has the axe in his hand, which he offers to Darius. Darius takes it and strikes the old man. But he does not move. He remains still. Darius approaches him and lifts his head. He is laughing. Laughing. The granddaughter dances in a tutu across the room. Now there is laughter everywhere. Darius strikes out again, but now the laughter multiplies until it is deafening.

Interval.

Darius wakes up. Silence in the flat. Sevgi is at the open door. He stares at her in horror.

Darius What time is it?

Sevgi It's just before five.

Darius Morning or afternoon?

Sevgi Afternoon. Are you all right?

Darius How did you find me?

Sevgi I asked around. They knew you from the bar. Are you ill?

Darius Why are you here?

Sevgi I wanted to thank you. Last night. I was drunk. I didn't thank you. And . . . here.

Darius What is it?

Sevgi Your money.

Darius Keep it.

Sevgi We're OK now.

Darius I don't want it.

Sevgi You've got to take it.

Darius I don't want it. How come you are suddenly OK?

Sevgi My mum borrowed some money.

Darius Who from?

Sevgi From a credit agency.

Darius Why will she take money from the agency but not from me?

Sevgi Just take it.

Darius Did you tell her where it came from? (*Beat.*) That's why. She doesn't want black money. And nor do you.

Sevgi That's not true.

Darius Then don't insult me. How much interest do those places charge? Twenty per cent? Twenty-five?

Sevgi It means we can keep going.

Darius It means you dig yourselves into a hole you can't get out of.

Sevgi You said you were rich. Why did you lie to me?

Darius Would you have taken it otherwise?

Sevgi No.

Darius People hate being helped. They'd rather be poor than grateful.

Sevgi I am grateful.

Darius You shouldn't be here.

Sevgi Because I am Turkish?

Darius No.

Sevgi Your friends might see me.

Darius I have no friends.

Sevgi Then your family.

Darius I have no family.

Pause.

Sevgi I'll go if you want. I'll go and you'll never see me again. Just say the word.

Pause.

I like you, Darius. You helped me, you didn't know who I was and you helped me. But you are sad. When I first saw you in the bar I looked at you for a long time and you didn't notice. I saw someone unhappier than me. I have problems, many problems, but you seem to be haunted by something.

Darius You should go back to your family.

Sevgi My family understands nothing of what goes on in my head.

Pause.

When you met me, I had a plan. I was going to drink as much as I possibly could, and then when I was down to my last coin I was going to go down to the canal. I was going to toss the coin. Heads I win. Tails the canal.

Darius You wouldn't have done it.

Sevgi You don't know that. There are people who are braver than others. People who see things through. I would have done it.

Pause.

Darius So now you don't have to quit college.

Sevgi Not yet. We have three weeks to find more money. But dad has disappeared. If he don't come back, I will have to work.

Darius I can get you more money.

Sevgi You don't have money.

Darius I can get it. I can go now.

Sevgi I don't want to take your money, you need it.

Darius I need it for nothing! That's why I got it, to free people like you! I want you to know something. It wasn't a race thing, no, maybe I thought it was, but it wasn't!

Sevgi What wasn't?

Darius It was for people like you, to take you out of this cycle . . .

Sevgi What cycle?

Darius Your mother works in the factory. How much does she earn?

Sevgi Two-fifty an hour.

Darius So when something goes wrong, as things do go wrong, you have to help out, so you work in the factory, two-fifty an hour, until like her you're withered and old. And then something goes wrong, you need help, and it will be the turn of younger sister – you have a younger sister?

Sevgi Leila.

Darius Then it will be Leila's turn, and then your daughter's, and her daughter's, and so it goes on, until someone dares to break it.

Darius goes down and kisses her foot.

Sevgi What are you doing?

Darius I am bowing to the whole of human suffering.

Sevgi What?

Darius (*laughs wildly*) I don't know, man. Maybe you should just throw yourself in the canal. And have done with it.

Sevgi Stop it.

Darius Why not go now? Get it over with! Because you will end up in the same sweatshop, and so will your sister and your daughter, and there's nothing any of you can do!

She slaps him. Pause.

Darius I'm sorry.

Sevgi Tell me what is troubling you.

Darius I can't.

She touches his face. She strokes his face. She kisses his face.

I can't.

Sevgi (*kissing him*) Don't be afraid. No one will find us.

Darius I can't.

Dawn the next day. Darius and Sevgi.

Sevgi My brothers will be looking for me.

Darius What will you tell them?

Sevgi I'll tell them I fell in the gutter. They're used to that. I have a reputation. A good Turkish girl doesn't drink, fuck, or think. I major on all three.

Darius What would they do if they knew?

Sevgi Depends. If I convinced them it was a one-night stand, they'd beat the shit out of me and leave it at that. But if I told them it was something else . . . something serious . . .

Darius Yes?

   Pause.

Sevgi Is it something more serious, Darius? Or were you just trying out a bit of Turkish?

Darius Listen. There's something.

Sevgi Yes?

Darius Something I haven't . . . You have to understand. I can tell you because we're the same.

Sevgi Why are we the same?

Darius Don't you get it?

Sevgi Get what?

Darius You said it yourself. Some people go the whole way. I've cut off from my family. From my friends. And you. By coming to me, by being with me, you've also crossed the line. You've committed a crime.

Sevgi I don't think so.

Darius But that's what they'll think. Your family, your friends.

Sevgi They won't ever know.

Darius They always know. And they'll come and they'll have their revenge. But we must take it – to break what must be broken. We must take the suffering upon ourselves. We have only each other. So let's take that path together.

Sevgi What path?

Darius That doesn't matter. As long as it's the same one. It's what must be done to be free. Freedom! Power!

Sevgi I don't understand.

Darius You have to go now.

Sevgi Why now?

Darius I have to be somewhere.

Sevgi Can't I come?

Darius I'll meet you tonight.

Sevgi Where?

Darius Down by the canal. There we can decide everything. All the avenues will be open to us then!

Sevgi What are you saying?

Darius If I don't come, then you'll hear about it yourself, and then you must remember what I said to you just now. Freedom. Power. But if I do come, I'll tell you something.

Sevgi Tell me what.

Darius I'll tell you who murdered your sister's friend.

Sevgi You know?

Pause.

Darius I was there. I saw. I have singled you out as the person I must tell. And I'll tell you. Get out of here. Don't kiss me. Until tonight!

Pause.

And Sevgi. Bring a coin.

Act Four

THE FALSE CONFESSION

The interview room. Campbell and Darius.

Campbell We seem to be having some difficulty finding your bracelet.

Darius I can come back later.

Campbell No no, since you've been so good as to come, it won't be a minute. Do you smoke? Please, take one. So impersonal these rooms, aren't they? I mean, they're all right for interrogations, but when we're just chatting. No air. (*Beat.*) I never really introduced myself, did I? Well it's a funny story, and since we have the time . . . You see, I used to be a big fish here. I was a detective inspector. I had a badge. I was good. I hope you'll forgive a moment's arrogance, but I was the dog's bollocks. But, was it the job, was it personal failing, I've thought about this so many times, the fact is over the years, I turned out rotten. There. I've said it. I became rotten inside, and I started to do rotten things. Maybe you can understand what it's like. One day, after a few years in the job, you have a case, a burglary, say. And you have a suspect. And because you've been around and you know a thing or two, you just know that the fella's as guilty as sin. But the evidence isn't there, you see. And the procedures you would need to go through to gather the evidence, the legal procedures, well they would be so lengthy and contorted, you'd never have time to solve another crime. So you 'find' the evidence in other ways. You create it. That's how it begins. Then you start to do the same with people you're not so sure

about, I mean maybe they didn't do that crime, but they
sure as hell did another and they're sure as hell going
to do another one soon. I had a couple of colleagues
who helped me. Bates and Devlin. I'm from Scotland,
Inverness originally, a lovely town, have you been there?
But they were both Londoners. Real Londoners if you
get my meaning. I noticed that the more we continued
with our little operation, the more it was black men we
were focusing on. I mentioned this to Bates one day.
He smiled at me and said I should see it as a clear-up
operation. 'Clearing the streets of the shit' is how he put
it. Then he asked me if I wanted in. I say asked. He
knew that by telling me about it, I was in. I became one
of the enforcers. It was simple and effective. Until Bates
was caught. They hushed it up, but Bates was sacked,
Devlin relocated. For some reason, maybe it was my age,
maybe it was sentiment, I was allowed to stay. I was
stripped of my rank, and told to spend my remaining
years behind a desk, filling forms and keeping my head
down.

Where is that girl with your things?

Darius I know what you're trying to do.

Campbell Hmmn?

Darius It's the oldest technique in the book: put the
suspect at their ease, open them up . . .

Campbell My dear fellow, we're just chatting while we
wait. Is it my strange laugh that unnerves you? You must
forgive me, it's a nervous tic, I've always been a rag-bag
of nerves. I used to drink. My wife and I split up twelve
years ago and I found myself spending every evening in
the Lansdowne. Don't touch the stuff now.

Darius I don't want to know about your problems.

Campbell Of course you don't, I was merely explaining my nervous laughter. Sometimes I wobble when I laugh. No, I do, it's on account of my strange shape. Excuse my walking up and down. I have piles, and I need to keep my exercise going. I'm thinking of going to the gym, but I can never quite convince myself. I'm embarrassed by my body is the truth. I know some of the officers do skipping. Yes. That's the problem with a desk job. Your arse suffers something awful. But it's interesting what you were saying. Putting the suspect at their ease. Very interesting. They don't do that any more. I don't know why. No time, no inclination. It's much more upfront these days. More confrontational. But sometimes, and asides from the aesthetics of it all, one does learn more from a friendly chat. Let me give you one example. Suppose I consider a person to be guilty of a crime, well, why, I ask, should I inconvenience the fellow before I need to? No really, I mean it quite seriously, say for example I were to haul this chap in, grill him like a sausage, in so doing I might actually be giving him moral support. And he'll go cold on me and withdraw into his shell and I'll learn nothing. Oh, I can see why you laugh.

Darius is not laughing.

It's a kind of psychobabble in a way. Of course it is. But what you have to understand is that every crime is a special case. I mean, there are some very strange examples of this special case. Sometimes it's really quite comical. Say I leave a certain young man alone. I don't arrest him, I don't trouble him, but I lay a seed of doubt that maybe, just maybe, I know. Then he does most of my work for me. He gets into a whirl, he starts to behave strangely, his nerves starts to take control of him.

What does he do? Well, let's say he goes to a party. But does he stay? No, he enters sweating like a pig, mutters some strange words no one can understand, and leaves.

Of course he could be ill. But it gives us a lead. Then on another occasion he'll play a little too cool, in a room such as this, he'll almost flirt with the idea of his own guilt with a member of the police force, a has-been clerk admittedly, but none the less, we can see the magnetism of his own crime working upon him. Are you warm? I can open a window.

Darius No.

Campbell Then he wanders back into the station, casual as you like, as if he is toying with us, when he would do well to stay clear as much as possible. Moth to a flame indeed!

Darius laughs. Campbell laughs. Both laugh merrily.

Darius Mr Campbell, it is clear to me now that you suspect me of the murder of the Turkish shopkeeper and his granddaughter. I am sick of your game-playing. If you have a shred of evidence, then, please, arrest me. But I will not allow you to laugh in my face like this.

Campbell But what is this?

Darius I won't allow it! Do you hear me?

Campbell Keep your voice down, please, young man. We don't want the whole station to hear.

Darius I won't allow it.

Campbell Listen, I have to say, you'll drive yourself crazy if you continue like this. I mean, I said as much to your friend when he came to see me last night.

Darius My friend . . .

Campbell Yes, he was very confused. He sat in this very room, and said nothing. I pointed out that he'd made the effort to come all the way here . . .

Darius What did he say?

Campbell He said you were ill. Well, we both agreed on that. And this illness, well this would account for everything, yes, I know about that. Well, of course it all fits in, you see, it all fits in perfectly. (*He laughs merrily.*)

Darius What does? Say it!

Campbell I had a case like this, 1984 I think it was, a young black man tried to pin a murder on himself, and my how he went about it. He was a depressive, you see, paranoid depressive. Luckily we saw through him. I've studied this a bit, this death-wish you might call it. It's an illness. A delirium.

Darius I am not ill!

Campbell Well, there you are! You see, if you had done all these things you're pinning on yourself, you would have accepted my excuse. How convenient it would have been for you! But no. You deny it. No, my dear fellow, you need medical help, and not some crappy GP, I suggest you see a psychiatrist without delay.

Darius This is just another part of your game.

Campbell There you go again. With that paranioa.

Darius All right. If you believe I am free from suspicion, let me go.

Campbell But your bracelet . . .

Darius Fuck my bracelet.

Campbell There you go, shouting again. My, what a job I'm having with you.

Darius I say it again. I can no longer endure . . .

Campbell The uncertainty?

Darius Stop tormenting me!

Campbell (*with deadly seriousness*) Keep your voice down! They hear you saying that, the whole thing will be blown open. You'll be let loose to the wolves!

> *Pause. Campbell's beeper goes off. Campbell exits, then re-enters, quite different, holding a tape.*

Darius What is it?

Campbell You're free to leave, Mr Jacobs.

Darius Why aren't you taking me to your friend?

Campbell Something's come up. Apologies for having taken up your time.

Darius I want to know what happened.

Campbell The case is closed.

Darius How?

> *Campbell puts the tape in the tape-player and plays. It is a young black man's voice, clearly deranged.*

Man's Voice I did it! I killed him with the axe and I killed the girl. I am the murderer! I am the murderer!

> *Pause.*

Darius Someone confessed?

Campbell They had him in for three days. It's good to see the old techniques are still in operation.

Darius (*laughs*) So I won't be seeing you again?

Campbell Well, it would seem so.

Darius No it is so! Where is my bracelet?

Campbell Oh yes. (*He takes it out of his pocket.*)

Darius Stick to the desk job.

Campbell Thank you for the advice. I'll be seeing you around, Mr Jacobs.

Darius' room. Darius alone.

Darius (*to a Campbell in his mind*) You have nothing on me. You needed my confession, that's why you came up with all that shit. The others have found their killer. They'll be happy with that. They won't ask any questions. You have nothing! (*to Sevgi, in his mind*) And her. Do I still have to tell her? I swore I would. But why should I? What's the use? But I swore I would. So the fuck what? She'll only hate me. She'll only hate herself. But I swore.

　A knock at the door. Raz enters.

Raz You fucking do that to me again I'll tear your tongue out with my hands and stick it on my wall. I nearly had a fucking heart attack, man. Giving me those wild eyes. Coming at me with that 'abandon me' shit. You screwing with my mind, man. I went to the fucking station, I was going to turn you in. I didn't sleep a wink for thinking about it. And now I find out they've found the little fucker that did it and you were just pissing me around!

Darius Accept it, man. You're a sucker.

Raz And you're a fucking lunatic, man. I am so fucking well out of that, man. I am breathing easy today. That look, man. You know you should go into movies, because that look was just evil! It was like pure wickedness and death in one gaze. Yuuugh! I don't want to think about it. You're doing it again, man! Get away from me. Get away!

Darius What's the problem?

Raz You're fucking deranged, that's the problem! You're a fucking nutcase and I don't know why I like you. And I don't even know if I do. And you know what I'm going to do now?

Darius Go and get high.

Raz Yes! Yes I am going to get off my fucking face, man, and no one's going to stop me. Because I have been living in my own little nightmare and I want to toast it being over. I want to fly to a place where I'm clear of the devils that are floating around your evil fucked-up head! So you coming or what?

Darius Later.

Raz Suit yourself. I'm not sure I could cope with getting high with you, anyway. You might spook me out.

Darius Raz. You're right not to want any part of me. Leave it for a while, don't trouble your head about it. Just go and get high.

Raz Yes, I will. Fuck you. I will go. I will go and get high.

The canal. Sevgi waiting. Darius enters but stays in the shadows.

Sevgi Darius. Is that you? Come into the light. I can't see you.

He comes into the light. She runs to hug him.

I thought you weren't coming back. I thought you were going to do something crazy.

Darius You thought I was going to kill myself?

Sevgi I don't know. I just . . .

Another shadow in the night. Sevgi's brother. Sevgi stops kissing Darius.

Brother (*in Turkish*) What are you doing, sister?

Sevgi What the fuck are you doing here? Go home! Leave me alone.

Brother (*in Turkish*) Who is he?

Sevgi None of your business.

Darius Who is he?

Sevgi I think maybe you should go.

Darius I'm not going anywhere.

Sevgi Why are you following me?

Brother (*to Darius*) What you doing talking to my sister?

Sevgi Don't touch him.

Brother (*to Sevgi, in Turkish*)) Get off me. I'll deal with you afterwards.

Sevgi Fuck you!

Brother What are you, a dealer or something?

Darius Just a friend.

Brother What kind of friend?

Darius I gave her some money to help her out.

Brother Why you give her money? You work for a charity or something?

Darius I like her.

Brother What do you mean? (*Pause.*) You're not . . . you're not . . .?

Sevgi You got a problem with that?

Brother You are the one with the problem. (*in Turkish*) You're coming home.

Sevgi No way.

Brother (*in Turkish*) I'm telling you, you're coming home now! (*Pause.*) Why can't you ever do what you are supposed to do? Find a proper Turkish boy.

Sevgi I know from my family too much what Turkish boys are like.

Brother (*in Turkish*) Don't insult your family.

Sevgi I don't give a fuck for my family.

Brother (*in Turkish*) Have some respect.

Sevgi Respect a man who gambles away his whole life? Respect a pair of brothers who are too busy fighting to earn any money!

Brother (*in Turkish*) How dare you talk to me like that? All your life I stop you getting into trouble. People say you are a wild animal, you're not to be trusted! I defend you! Now look what you do to me.

Sevgi I don't need no one to protect me.

Brother (*in Turkish*) We'll see about that.

Sevgi What does that mean?

Brother (*in Turkish*) It means what I say. I have given you your chance.

Darius What is he saying?

Sevgi He is threatening me. He says he has protected me long enough.

Darius From what?

Sevgi You know what they do to Turkish girls who fuck black boys? They beat them, they cut them. Sometimes they set them on fire. Don't you, brother?

Brother You will never see my sister again.

Darius It's not your business.

   Beat.

Brother What you say?

Darius You are not free to tell her what to do.

Brother What did you say?

Darius You are not free. You have no power. You are weak and you are scared of those who are strong. Your sister is stronger than you. And you hate her for it.

Brother Be careful now.

Darius She is free and you want to cage her.

Brother Shut up. Shut the fuck up! (*He holds a knife in the darkness.*)

Sevgi Don't you dare touch him!

Darius Go on, then. Kill me.

   Pause.

It's bad luck for you, but you are looking at a man who has no fear. You weren't to know that.

Brother I'm warning you.

Darius I read a book once, and it said that there was nothing so dangerous as a man with nothing to lose.

Brother I'm giving you a chance to get out of here.

Darius And I'm not moving.

The Brother lunges towards Darius but Sevgi gets between them.

Sevgi I'll come home! Give me five minutes. I'll come home.

Pause.

Brother Five minutes.

He runs off down the towpath dialling on his phone.

Sevgi Let's go. He'll be back with my brothers. We can't stay here.

Darius In a minute.

Sevgi Don't be crazy.

Darius In a minute.

Pause.

Sevgi What's wrong with you?

Pause.

What is it?

Darius It's all right, Sevgi. Don't be frightened. It's just a pile of shit. In the end it really is shit if you give it any thought. But why have I come to torment you? In the end. Why?

Sevgi What is it?

Darius It's all shit! (*Beat.*) You remember this morning. On your way out, I said I might be saying goodbye, but that if I came back tonight, I would tell you . . . who killed your sister's friend.

Pause.

Well, so I've come to tell you.

Sevgi I thought they'd found him. It was on the radio. A man confessed.

Darius They haven't found him.

Sevgi How do you know?

Darius I just know.

Sevgi But how?

Pause.

Darius Guess.

Pause.

Sevgi Why are you frightening me like this?

Darius You see, he didn't mean to kill your sister's friend. He . . . killed her . . . by accident. He meant to kill the old man . . . when he was alone . . . and he went there . . . but then your sister's friend came in . . . so he killed her . . . too.
So you can't guess, then?

Sevgi N-no.

Darius Then take a good look.

Pause.

Have you guessed?

Sevgi crumples against the wall of the towpath.

141

Sevgi No. No. I don't believe you.

She recoils from him. She seems to be about to be sick. Then she turns back to look at him. Then she moves to him and seizes both his hands and stares into his face. Suddenly she believes him.

Oh God. Oh God. Oh God!

Darius Just go. Don't torture me any more.

Sevgi suddenly starts to beat at him with her fists. He does not resist.

Sevgi What have you done? What have you done to yourself?

Suddenly she embraces him for dear life.

Darius You're a funny one. You put your arms around me and kiss me after I've told you a thing like that.

Sevgi pushes him away.

Sevgi Fuck you. Fuck you! Why? Why did you do that? How could you, a man like you, do a thing like this?

Darius I did it so I could rob her.

Sevgi No. No no no. There must be another reason.

Darius Why must there?

Sevgi Was it . . . his money you gave me? Oh God. Oh God!

Darius It wasn't.

Sevgi It was!

Darius It was money sent to me. I thought I would give you more from his bags later but I didn't have time. I don't even know if I stole any money. I hid it in a locker without even looking at it.

Sevgi So why did you say you did it to rob him, if you didn't take anything?

Darius (*maliciously*) I may still take that money.

Sevgi Don't fuck with me!

Darius And if I could do that, then imagine what I could do to you here, now.

Sevgi Stop it. Stop it.

Darius I didn't do it for the money. Oh, I can't explain. It will only make you suffer more. Why did I tell you? Why did I come here? Just go. Please. Go!

Sevgi I have to know why you did it.

Darius Because I wanted to free the black race.

Sevgi You what?

Darius The law is the white man's. He owns it, he creates it, he changes it when it suits him, and so long as it benefits him he obeys it. Then he gets the black man to live by it too.

Sevgi But that man was not white.

Darius He was worse than white. He was the white man's bailiff. He did the dirty work, keeping us down, keeping us in our rightful place! His riches were bought with the freedom of a hundred black men.

Sevgi He was not rich!

Dorian He had it coming!

Sevgi No, that's wrong. That's wrong.

Darius To kill an old man! And his innocent grand-daughter? Of course it is wrong! It's worse than wrong! But it was true to my beliefs.

Sevgi What kind of truth is that?

Darius I killed a rat! A worthless rat!

Sevgi A human being.

Darius Oh, I know he wasn't really a rat. Actually I'm talking shit. I've been doing that for a long time now. The real reasons are different. Totally fucking different. Man, I haven't spoken to anyone for a long time. My head . . .

Sevgi But how could you? How could you?

Darius Because I'm evil! I'm deranged and insane and wicked and callous and all the words they used in the paper. I am a malicious spider, I hid away in my shit-pit of a room, spinning crazy ideas in my crazy fucked-up head. I lay there for days on end, not eating, not drinking, just thinking, what dreams I had, no point trying to tell you, and then I began to imagine . . . no that's not right, you see how hard it is to explain! I kept asking myself, 'Why am I so stupid? Why is it that if others are stupid, if for example my mother is stupid, and I know she is stupid, then I don't make myself cleverer?' And I realised I was sitting waiting for the black race to become cleverer, for all my friends to see what I could see, that this is all just a con. We're being conned into believing that everything is made for us, and then I realised that if I was going to wait for everyone else to become cleverer, I'd die waiting, and that I would have to do it myself. And then, Sevgi listen to me! Then I understood that power, freedom only come to those who dare to stoop to pick it up! Yes! Those who dare!

Sevgi Stop it. Stop it, please.

Darius Sevgi, shut it, please. Shut it. I didn't kill for money, or for others, or for justice, or for race. No, I killed for myself. I needed to know whether I was a rat or a man. Whether I could take the step across. If you're George W. Bush, and you want to take that step, it's easy, you just accept a bribe, take a backhander, stitch up a rival. But when you're me, a black man in Dalston, then taking the step is hard. It may involve killing. I had to decide that I had the right to kill.

Sevgi Whether you had the right?

Darius Oh, for God's sake, can't you see? I did it and only then did I find out it was the devil talking in my ear! Because I don't have the right! I am just a rat, otherwise these thoughts wouldn't still be ripping through my head. I can't get it out of my soul! That's the blackest part of the joke. Did I really kill the old man? No, it was myself I killed! It was myself.

Pause.

What should I do? I came here because I needed you to tell me what I should do. Throw myself in the water? I will if you say so. Give myself up? I will.

Sevgi You can't stay here. My brothers will be back soon.

Darius Where do I go? Tell me, Sevgi.

Sevgi Go home.

Darius Not there. I can't.

Sevgi Just for tonight. And tomorrow, leave.

Darius Leave for where?

Sevgi Anywhere. We'll catch a train. We'll take it as far as it can take us. No one will come after us. They think they have the killer.

Darius You're coming with me? You don't want revenge. Justice, for what I did?

Sevgi What good would it do?

Darius But I split their heads open with an axe.

Sevgi You were poor. You were crazy.

Darius And you don't hate me?

Pause.

Sevgi I don't hate you, Darius.

Darius Where shall we meet?

Act Five

THE CONFESSION

Midnight. Darius alone in his flat. He has a travelling bag and is putting a few things in it. Not that there is much to pack.

He finds a Bible deep under a pile of clothes. He opens it and reads the inscription in the inner sleeve.

Voice of Mother Dear Darius. Wishing you all of God's gifts on your life in London. May it bring you true happiness. Your loving mother.
'And whosoever liveth and believeth in me, shall not perish but have everlasting . . .'

But Darius closes the Bible and throws it away. The door opens.

Campbell Going somewhere, Mr Jacobs?

Darius What are you doing here?

Campbell You know I came earlier but you were out. You left your door open. You shouldn't do that. There are some dangerous people round here.

Darius Have you got a warrant?

Campbell Oh I'm not here in an official capacity. No, I just thought I'd pop round for a quick chat before you go.

Darius Go where?

Campbell You tell me. (*He lights a cigarette.*) They do me nothing but harm these cigarettes. But I can't quit. I'm short of breath just from walking up those stairs.

I went to see a doctor about it. He tapped my chest a
few times and burst out laughing.

Oh yes, Darius I understand self-destruction.

Well of course you're wondering what I'm doing here,
and the answer is that I've come to explain myself. We
have our man now, which is a great relief to everybody,
but it does mean I am obliged to offer you an explanation.
I think it my duty to do so after all I put you through.

I'm not a monster, Darius, I understand how hard it
must be to carry all this on a man's shoulders when he's
depressed, but also proud and masterful and impatient.
Yes, above all impatient! Well, I consider you a man of
the most noble character, with even the beginnings of a
true greatness of soul. But you're a funny one, Darius.
Playing that trick on your mate, convincing him you did
it, what for? Cruel pleasure? To test him? But why? And
why come back to me so readily when you knew I was
one of those irritating types who can't let go of the scent
once he's got a whiff of it? That's that arrogance of
yours. It's a flaw, if I may say so. And then when I found
out that they'd forced a confession out of that other sad
bastard, the look of triumph on your face. Well, I can
understand. It seemed then to you that you were in the
clear. It must have seemed so.

Darius Seemed?

Campbell Seemed, yes.

Darius But it is. He has confessed.

Campbell Yes, he has.

Darius What does that mean?

Campbell You know he's a funny little fella, that one.
What is he, seventeen, total fucking tearaway, spends
half his life on crack, the other driving cars into walls.
A total fucking child. Between you and me, I don't think

he's all there in the head. Oh, he has imagination, but it's
wild, it's frightening. He's very proud of his confession.
I spoke to him earlier. Loved talking about the blood.
The gore. The axe. Loved the axe. The problem with
him is he has no detail. Oh, he did his best. But no detail
at all. No, he's not our man. I imagine he'll retract his
confession pretty soon, and then what? They might force
it through, Christ we need a fucking answer to this one,
this one is top priority on the political-correctness chart.
But he's not our man. He's not our man.

Darius Then. Who is?

Campbell Who is? Why, you are. You are the murderer,
Darius. Have you not understood? I've come here to get
everything out in the open.

   Pause.

Darius It wasn't me. I didn't do it.

Campbell Yes, Darius it was you, you and no one else.

Darius Prove it.

Campbell Oh, I don't need proof. In my own mind, I am
convinced.

Darius So why come here? Why not get them to arrest
me?

Campbell Well firstly they wouldn't believe me. No, I
will need evidence, and I think I should get it quite soon.
We simply need to find the bag of stuff you've hidden,
you've probably hidden it in a station locker-room or a
sports hall, something like that. Secondly, I am sincerely
fond of you, Darius. And so I have come here with a
proposal.

Darius What proposal?

Campbell I want you to give yourself up. It would be a whole lot better for you, and for me too. Well, what do you say?

Darius What if you're mistaken?

Campbell I'm not mistaken. You see, when I said I don't have evidence, it may be that I have some access to evidence . . . (*He holds out the key to the locker.*) I've worked in this job for a long time, Darius. I have learnt a great deal about people, about why people do what they do. Now I am approaching the end of my time. I want to help someone before I go. It will be so much better for you if you confess now. Imagine. They have a man already in the cells for this, but you choose to give yourself up! You show remorse, you show dignity, you make the whole thing seem like a moment of madness. Have you any idea how different that will seem to the courts? That's worth five, ten years at least. Now listen to me. No one at the station knows about this. No one! I swear to God that if you do this, I will make it look as if your confession was completely unexpected. You'll hear nothing from me, I will just continue processing forms in my office and I'll leave it all up to them. I'm a decent man, Darius, I will keep my word.

Darius Why are you doing this?

Campbell Christ, we all need to be forgiven, Darius.

Darius I don't want it! I don't want your kindness.

Campbell Ah. That was what I was afraid of.

Pause.

Don't throw away your life, son. You've still got a great deal ahead of you.

Darius A great deal of what?

Campbell What are you scared of? Is it bad for your cred to give yourself in?

Darius I don't give a fuck about that!

Campbell So what, then? You don't think you deserve it? Listen, you had a theory, a theory about race, about social conditions, a theory that turned out to be full of shite and fucked-up. But you're not evil. You know what I think you are? You're the sort of man who if he was having his guts ripped out would stand looking at his torturers with a smile, so long as he'd found a faith. You need something to believe in. Isn't that really what you want? Well, keep searching!

Darius What are you, some kind of prophet?

Campbell Oh, me, I'm just a man who's had his day. A man who may have feelings, may be capable of sympathy, but who has most certainly had his day. But you. You're the future. You have a life to live. OK, so you'll be locked up for some of it. You're not exactly going to miss your creature comforts, are you?

Darius When are you going to arrest me?

Campbell I thought I'd give you two days. Give you a chance to run away if you want to. But I advise you very strongly against it. I don't think you would suit a life on the run, Darius. No, you must choose to suffer. Suffering is a great thing, Darius. I know, look at me, fat old white git, what do I know? But I can tell you, from my heart, suffering has a purpose.

Well, I have to be up early in the morning.

Darius I've confessed nothing.

Campbell Oh, I know. It's out of my hands now. Either way I don't suppose I shall see you again. I shan't ask you to shake my hand. Good luck, Mr Jacobs, in whatever you decide.

Good luck, son.

Exit Campbell. Pause. Darius reaches for the phone, dials.

Darius Mum. It's me. You're probably asleep. I'm just calling to tell you that I've going away. For ever. You're going to be unhappy, Mum. But you must remember that all the things you thought about me, that I made you think, that I'm cruel and don't love you, all those things are false. I'll never ever stop loving . . . (*He slams the phone down.*)

Euston Station. Eight-fifteen in the morning. Sevgi waiting with bags. Enter Darius with bag.

Sevgi I thought you weren't coming. I've bought the tickets.

Darius Where d'you get the money?

Sevgi I stole my mother's purse. We're going to Liverpool, I have a friend who studies there. She's agreed to put us up for a while.

What is it?

Darius I've never been to Liverpool.

Sevgi We don't have to stay there. It's just a start.

Darius Yeah, it's just a start.

Sevgi What's wrong?

Darius Nothing. Let's go.

Sevgi What?

Darius Nothing.

Sevgi Darius, listen to me. I have more right to hate you than you do. Stop punishing yourself. Here's your ticket. (*Pause.*) Darius, the train leaves in five minutes.

Darius I know.

Sevgi So come on.

Darius I'm coming.

Sevgi We don't have time for this. Move!

Darius I'm coming.

Sevgi Come on then. What is it?

Darius I don't know.

Sevgi Darius, please.

Darius I'm coming.

Sevgi Then move! (*Drags him.*) Darius, people are looking at us.

Darius I'm coming.

Sevgi Then come on. Walk. Walk!

Darius starts to walk, half-carried by Sevgi. Then he suddenly crumples on the floor.

Get up. Get the fuck up! (*to people around*) He's fine. He's just drunk. What's so fucking interesting? Haven't you ever seen a drunk person before?

She lifts him, they make a few more feet, then he crumples again.

Get up. Get up! (*to people*) I don't want your help! Just leave us fucking alone! (*to Darius*) Get up! (*to people*) You got a problem? Then stop staring at me! Get on with your life! Go to work! (*to Darius*) The train's going. Darius, I can't carry you! Come on! Please walk! Please! Please!

She lifts him with an almighty effort, then collapses over him in tears. Pause. Darius laughs.

Darius You know what fucks me off? The thought that those same bastards who tried to frame that poor innocent fucker will take all the credit for this.

Sevgi What?

Darius No one will know about Campbell.

Sevgi What are you talking about?

Pause.

Darius I'm giving myself up.

Sevgi No you're not!

Darius It's right.

Sevgi It's not! Get on the train, we can talk about it on the train.

Darius I have to go now.

Sevgi Get on the fucking train! (*Beat.*) You can't. You can't leave me.

Darius I have to.

Sevgi You bastard! What will I do? What the fuck will I do?

Darius Go on your own. Maybe it's better that way.

Sevgi How can you say that? You fucking arsehole! I'm staying with you.

Darius You know you can't do that. Think about your family. Your brothers . . .

Sevgi I don't care what they do to me. I'm staying with you.

Darius Now you listen. I don't want you to have nothing to do with it.

Sevgi I love you.

Darius I don't want your love! You hear me? I don't want it! I want your hate. I want to suffer alone and hate alone and be alone for all time!

Why are you crying? (*to the station*) Why is she crying? Will someone tell me why she is crying! (*to Sevgi*) Listen. Stop loving me! Forget me! Leave me alone!

Sevgi You have no right to tell me what to do. My love is mine alone to give.

> *She approaches him and tries to kiss his head. He evades. She tries again. He evades still.*

(*to the station*) I love this man! You hear me? I love this man!

Darius I have to go.

Sevgi I'm coming with you.

Darius I don't want you.

Sevgi I'm coming with you.

Darius I don't . . .

Sevgi I'm coming.

Darius Don't.

Sevgi I'm coming.

Stoke Newington police station. Darius. Behind him, Sevgi.

Darius I need to speak to whoever is in charge of the murder investigation. The investigation into the murder in the shop. Yes. Is he here? Could I speak to him, please? Yes, I'll wait.

> *Pause. Darius glances at Sevgi. A figure in the doorway.*

Yes. My name is Darius Jacobs. I simply wanted. I just wanted to say. I'm the person. I'm the person who murdered the old Turkish shopkeeper and his granddaughter. I did it with an axe and I robbed them.

> *Pause.*

I'm the person who murdered the old Turkish shopkeeper and his granddaughter. I did it with an axe and I robbed them.

> *The End.*

THE NATIVITY

for Bessie and Claude

The Nativity was first performed at the Young Vic Theatre on 22 November 1999. The cast was as follows:

Caspar Sarah Theresa Belcher
Abraham Dave Fishley
Balthazar Kate Fleetwood
Joseph Toby Jones
Benjamin Dominic McHale
Melchior Sabina Netherclift
Herod Toby Sedgwick
The Devil Nicholas Sidi
Mary Nina Sosanya

Other parts played by members of the company

Director David Farr
Designer Angela Davies
Music Paul Clark
Lighting Adam Silverman
Puppetry Sue Buckmaster
Script Editor Simon Reade
Sound Crispian Covell
Musical Instruments David Sawyer
Illusions Paul Kieve
Assistant Director Craig Higginson

Characters

Joseph
Villagers
Village Children
Mary
Mary's Father
Aaron
Wedding Guests
Bridesmaids
Mary and Joseph's Donkey
Beggar/Gabriel
Herod
Herod's Serving Girl
Minister of Justice
Waterseller
Abraham
Sarah
Isaac
Isaac's Midwives
Two Trusty Men
God
Talking Bush
Goliath
David
Warriors
Solomon
Officer
Two Prostitutes
Market Traders
The Devil (Old Man)
The Devil's Men

Ezra the Innkeeper
Three Shepherds
Benjamin the Mad Shepherd
Benjamin's Mad Sheep
Spies
Caspar
Melchior
Balthazar
Herod's Commander
Soldiers

Act One

ONE: THE ANNUNCIATION

A man. A poor man. Forty years old. Quiet, dignified,
but resigned.
  Joseph the carpenter.

A Voice in the Dark Joseph loved wood.

  Wood falls from the sky, scattering around Joseph.
  He starts to work.
    A circle of Villagers gathers to watch him.

Villagers Joseph lived in a small village in one of the
most remote northern districts of Galilee. The land was
poor, the sun baked down, rain almost never fell. The
men worked the barren fields to produce what food they
could for their families. The women slaved at home,
making the most of the meagre crop. The children wore
simple clothes and built their toys from whatever they
could find. But once a year they would receive a special
toy from Joseph the carpenter.

  The tools of the shop make music as he works.
  A group of Children.

Child 1 Joseph? Will you make me a toy?

Child 2 Joseph, will you make me one too?

Child 3 Joseph. Will you make me a toy?

Child 4 And me!

Child 5 And me!

Child 6 And me!

Joseph He built toys for all the children in the district!

Villager But other people's children. Joseph the carpenter had no children of his own.

A family rush in. Joseph presents them with a beautiful wooden kite.

Mother Thank you, Joseph. It's beautiful.

Girl Why aren't you married, Joseph?

Mother Sshhh, Leah. That is none of your business.

They leave, the girl flying the kite which soars into the air. Joseph watches sadly as she plays with the kite.

Joseph Joseph was forty years old and still he had no wife. His brothers had wives, his friends had wives and children. Beautiful children. But Joseph did not.
Because when it came to women, Joseph was unbelievably . . . shy!

Joseph and a girl, eighteen. The girl likes Joseph.

Girl Hello, Joseph. How are you?

Joseph . . .

The girl waits a while as Joseph struggles to speak, then she yawns and runs away with another young man. Joseph hits himself in despair.

Joseph had resigned himself to never falling in love!

Villager And then, one day . . .

A storm breaks over the village. The scene dissolves. The rain pours. Clouds fly across the sky. Great wind and rain pour from the heavens.

Village Boy A storm broke over the village. The wind poured dark clouds across the sky and rain fell in torrents! No one had ever seen a storm like it!

An Old Man (*to his grandson*) It is a message of anger from God! Hurry inside and close the shutters!

The shutters of all the village bang shut against the wind and rain. Clack. Clack. Clack.
A beautiful girl. Caught in the rain. Running home. She is fifteen. Feisty and free-spirited. She is Mary. She is soaked to the bone.

Mary A young girl was caught playing in the pouring rain. She loved it! But then she got cold. She was far from her cottage and could find no shelter. (*She seeks the nearest shelter but everywhere is barred up.*) Let me in! Let me in!
Finally she found an open door. Inside was a shop filled with wonderful things. She remembered it from her childhood. But it was the first time she had been inside for years!

Joseph It was Joseph's shop.

It is Joseph's shop. He is alone amidst the fruits of his life's work. Mary enters.
Joseph is carving a piece of wood. He looks at her fearfully.

Mary May I wait inside until the storm is over?

Joseph . . .

Joseph nods awkwardly. He returns to his work. Mary stands politely.

Joseph had never seen such a beautiful girl in all his life. He was terrified!

Mary You must be Joseph.

Joseph . . .

Mary I am Mary.

Joseph . . .

Mary laughs and dances round the room.

Mary What are you making?

Joseph Oh. It's a . . . a . . .
All of a sudden, Joseph had forgotten the word for
what he was making!
It's a . . . a . . .

Mary A chair?

He shakes his head.

A bed?

No, not a bed. Joseph mimes it.

Maybe a shelf? A bookcase?

Joseph No! It's a . . .

Mary A bench! A stool! A table!

Joseph Yes! A table. A table!

Mary Mary liked the man. He was different to the boys
who were always chasing her and trying to impress her.
(*She comes closer.*) How many tables have you made?

Joseph A lot.

Mary As many as there are stars in the sky?

Joseph More.

Mary As many as there are grains of sand in the desert?

Joseph More!

Mary Show me your hands.

Joseph shows her his hands. She touches them.

When Mary touched the carpenter's hands, a strange
feeling awoke in her.

Joseph When Joseph felt the girl's young hands on his, he knew he had fallen in love.

The pots in Joseph's kitchen sing.
Still Mary holds Joseph's hands. She finds them quite beautiful.

Mary They looked at each other as the storm raged!

Joseph The look seemed to last an eternity!

Mary Mary waited for him to say something! Anything!

Joseph But Joseph was struck dumb.

The storm passes.

Mary The storm has passed.

Joseph Yes.

Mary I must go.

Joseph . . .
And she left!
No, come back! I love you completely and utterly and I want to marry you.
Too late. She's gone!
For three whole days, Joseph did nothing but think of the girl. For the first time in his life he couldn't work properly! He made tables with legs of different heights, chairs with only three legs! He talked to the hammer as if it were her. He held nails like they were her fingers!
I love you. I love you. Marry me!

Mary Mary rushed to her room and tried to forget this fateful meeting. But all she could dream of was him. Days passed! Interminable days!
Why doesn't he come?

Joseph Joseph was in turmoil!
I could go to her father and ask for her hand. But she will certainly reject me!

Mary Mary was sick with love! She locked the door of her room and determined to starve until he came!

Joseph I will not go!

Mary He must come!

Joseph But all I can think of is her! What should I do? Finally he could bear it no more!

The Father arrives.

He rushed to the house of her father and knocked! I am here to ask for the hand of . . . of . . .

An agonising silence as Joseph fails to say the name of his beloved. Then, thankfully . . .

Mary's Father Say it, Joseph, and she is yours. She has been waiting for you.

Flowers fall. Joseph hugs Mary.

Villagers Three months later they were married! The whole village brought flowers and fruit to celebrate this strange union!

No one could believe it. Joseph the carpenter, who couldn't speak to a girl without falling over, married, and to the most beautiful girl in the village!

A wedding banquet.

Mary's Father Mary's father gave a long and heartfelt speech . . . (*He gives a long speech during which people fall asleep.*)

Aaron And Joseph's brother spoke of Joseph as a good and kind man who would make Mary very happy.

Applause.

Guest There was drinking and dancing!

Music and a dance.

Another Guest And magic tricks!

Magic tricks.

Another Guest And jokes!

Jokes.

Another Guest And everyone got wonderfully merry!

Drunken walking.

Joseph Except Mary. She seemed distracted. (*to her*) What is wrong my love? This is the happiest day of my life. But your face is clouded by a worry. Do you wish you had not married me?

Mary It's not that. I will tell you when we are alone.

The party disappears.

Joseph We are alone. Now tell me.

Mary I cannot come to your bed tonight as a wife should.

Joseph If you need time, take it. I have waited long enough, I can wait another day.

Mary I may not come then either.

Joseph Then when? How long must I wait? I want to have a child with you.

Mary staggers and falls.

What is it?

Mary I feel sick. Dizzy. (*She weeps.*)

Joseph Tell me. Whatever it is I will love you for ever.

Mary turns. She smiles a radiant smile.

Mary You will?

Joseph Yes, my love!

Mary Then know. I am pregnant.

A shutter slams in the night.

Joseph Joseph was chilled to the core of his being. His wife, pregnant with another man's child on the day of his wedding!
Whose is it? What trick have you played on me?

Mary It is no man's.

Joseph You want me to raise another man's child! You know what the law says. A woman who is caught being unfaithful will be stoned!

Mary It is no man's!

Joseph I will annul the marriage and hide you in the mountains where your shame will be kept secret from the village. Although you have betrayed and misused me I do not wish you to come to any harm. I love you too much.

Mary Joseph! Do you believe?

Joseph Yes of course.

Mary Then listen and believe!
I was in my room preparing for the wedding day . . .

Bridesmaids (*rushing in*) With your bridesmaids!

Mary When a beggar man came knocking.

Beggar Charity!

Bridesmaids Away, dirty rat! This is a wedding day!

Beggar Charity!

Bridesmaid Away, scoundrel, before I pour water on your head!

Beggar Charity!

The bridesmaids proceed to pour water over his head. But the water misses him and they soak each other instead.

Bridesmaids Aaah! You've ruined our dresses! Get out! Get out!

Mary No, wait. Come in. (*to the bridesmaids*) Fetch me my bag.

The Bridesmaids run out.

We were left alone. His clothes were old and he smelt of rotten grass and foul water. But his eyes kept staring at me. Then he spoke.

Beggar I am the Angel Gabriel.

Mary (*giggling*) You're who?

Beggar I am the Angel Gabriel.

Mary Hello. I'm the Queen of Sheba!

The Beggar transforms into an angel. The windows clatter and sing.

Mary Oh my.

Gabriel You have a child in your belly. It is the child of God. In nine months you will give birth. Until that time, your husband may not sleep with you. For yours will be a virgin birth. And your child will be the newborn King, born to rule over Israel.
   This is your fate. Believe.

Mary I believe.

Bridesmaids The bridesmaids returned!

Mary I rushed to show them the angel!
But only the beggar remained.

Beggar Charity!

Joseph The story is impossible! Madness. But your eyes speak truth. My reason says your story must be false. My heart says it is true. Which is right? (*He walks out under the moon.*) Joseph ran out of the room and walked under the moon and cried out.
My reason tells me one thing but my heart another! Which is right? Is it true what she says?

The Leaves of the Trees The wind rose and spoke to him through the leaves of the lemon trees.
True. True.

Joseph What? What did you say?

The Leaves of the Trees True. True.

The Birds in the Trees True! True!

Joseph But I need proof!

The Beggar passes through the trees.

Beggar He who needs proof is damned.

Joseph Who are you?

But the Beggar disappears.

And nature spoke to him in all its glory!

Nature in All its Glory Believe!

Joseph runs into his house and kneels before Mary.

Joseph Forgive me. I believe you. And I love you!

Mary I love you!

And Mary's belly grows like magic as . . .

TWO: THE ROAD TO BETHLEHEM

. . . Herod is carried in on a richly clothed couch in his palace of gold, his feet being massaged by Serving Girls.

Herod's Serving Girls Eight months later!

Herod In his luxurious and spacious palace in the heart of Jerusalem, King Herod was anxiously awaiting some important news.

Distant screaming rises and fades. Herod listens intently.

Minister of Justice (*entering*) My lord.

Herod What news, Minister of Justice?

Minister of Justice The men who tried to assassinate you this morning have been caught, fairly tried, tortured and executed.

Herod Very good. Did they confess?

Minister of Justice No, my lord. They maintained a total silence, only opening their mouths to curse you as a corrupt and despotic tyrant.

Herod Liars! Traitors!

Minister of Justice At least now you may sleep easy in your bed.

Herod (*relaxing*) Ah yes. Sweet sleep! (*then worried again*) But what if others try the same thing? You are my Minister of Justice. This must never happen again!

Minister of Justice My lord, it would be easier to police the people if we knew who they were and where they lived.

Herod But there are so many of the little rats. How would we do that?

Minister of Justice Command everyone in the country to register for a census.

Herod Brilliant! I will do so immediately.

Herod turns and speaks to his people (the audience).

I am issuing the following decree. A census of the population will take place one month from today. Every man and woman in the land must travel to . . . to . . . (*He sticks his finger on the royal map at random and plucks a name.*) Bethlehem! And register. No one is exempt! Young and old. The healthy and the lame. The blind and insane. All must proceed to Bethlehem. This is the word of the King!

In the village, Mary is heavily pregnant. She heaves a saddle-pack towards the waiting donkey.

Joseph Joseph and Mary borrowed a donkey from Mary's father.

Mary The road to Bethlehem was over a hundred miles. Mary's back hurt from the weight of the baby and she dreaded the journey.
Do we have to go now?

Joseph It is the word of the King.

They set off, Joseph leading. The sun rises.

The Samarian desert stretched out before them. The sun beat down above them. All around them: emptiness.

Mary On the first day they were jaunty and full of enthusiasm.

Joseph On the second day they were determined and full of confidence.

Mary On the third day they were resilient and full of fine words.

Joseph On the fourth day they were tired but happy.

Mary On the fifth day they ran out of food.

Joseph On the sixth day they ran out of water.

Mary On the seventh day they collapsed . . .

They fall to the ground, exhausted.
    A poor Waterseller woman appears.

Waterseller . . . by the side of the road.
    Where are you heading, strangers?

Joseph To Bethlehem.

Mary To register for the census.

Joseph Word of the King.

Mary Who are you?

Waterseller I am a waterseller.

Mary A waterseller! Oh please, please, give us water . . .

Joseph We need water . . .

Mary We have been travelling for seven days and our supply has run out.

Waterseller I have none.

Joseph What?

Waterseller There has been no rain for eight months. The well is dry.

Mary No water? But I have to have water for the child!

They look around them in despair.

Are we to die here?

Joseph Why would God be so cruel?

Mary Maybe we have done something to anger him.

Joseph Maybe we are not good enough.

Mary Maybe he has abandoned us.

Joseph Maybe he has left us to die.

  Pause.

Waterseller Dear friends, you seem disheartened. Let me tell you a story that will restore your faith.

  Abraham appears. An old man. Small, terribly thin, but upright. Inscrutable.

Long ago in this land there lived a good man. He was called Abraham.

  Sarah, his wife, appears.

And he had a wife called Sarah. She was old and beyond child-bearing age. But God visited her and gave her a child.

The Village A miracle!

  Sarah gives birth to Isaac.

Midwives A boy! They called him Isaac. He grew into a healthy lad.

  The Waterseller becomes Isaac.

Sheep One day, Abraham was tending his sheep when God spoke to him.

God Here I am.

Abraham My God, what do you want of me?

God You have a son, Isaac. Take him to the holy mountain and burn him as a sacrifice.

Sheep Abraham did not ask why, but said:

Abraham I will do as you ask, my Lord.

Sheep Sarah burst into tears and tried to hold on to Isaac.

Sarah Do not take him! He is our only son!

Abraham Trust God.

Isaac Where are we going, Father?

Abraham We are going to sacrifice a lamb on the holy mountain.

Trusty Man 1 He took two trusty men and travelled to the mountain. Then Abraham said to his men.

Abraham Wait here for me. I will return.

Trusty Man 2 Father and son climbed. Abraham carried the wood for the fire.

They climb the mountain.

As they were climbing, Isaac the boy asked:

Isaac Father, I see the wood to burn. And the tinder to create fire. But where is the lamb we are sacrificing? I don't see it.

Trusty Man 1 And Abraham replied . . .

Abraham God will provide the lamb.

Trusty Man 2 And Abraham remained noble, but Isaac became afraid.

Isaac I still do not see the lamb we are to sacrifice, Father.

Abraham God will provide the lamb.

Trusty Man 1 They reached the top of the mountain.

Isaac I still do not see the lamb.

Trusty Man 1 Abraham looked to the sky.

Trusty Man 2 Silence.

Abraham sighs a deep sigh of sorrow.

Abraham I must tie you down.

Isaac No!

He ties his screaming son to the wood and lays him on the altar.

Trusty Man 1 Then Abraham took a knife from his belt.

Trusty Man 2 And held it aloft above the head of his son.

Isaac No!

Trusty Man 1 No!

Joseph No!

Trusty Man 2 No!

Mary No!

Abraham puts the knife to his son's neck.
A mad screaming.
Sudden clap of thunder. Darkness. Then light. Isaac is free. A ram has replaced him.
Abraham holds his son, shaking with emotion.

Abraham Thank you, my God.

Waterseller Faith is like water. Without it we wither and die. Because Abraham had faith he was rewarded. And his son Isaac grew old and wise and gave birth to Jacob, after whom this well is named.

Another clap of thunder. The Waterseller dances. Rain falls on Joseph and Mary. They drink together and are jubilant. They dance in the rain.

Mary The heavens opened and a great rain fell! They drank at Jacob's Well!

They continue, Joseph leading purposefully.

Joseph In two weeks they crossed the Samarian desert.

Mary And reached the great stone mountains of the interior.
Joseph?

Joseph Yes, my love.

Mary Can we go round the mountains?

Joseph No, we have to go over them.

Mary (*looking at the most enormous of the mountains*) And that highest one whose peak seems to pierce the sky – do we have to climb that one?

Joseph There is no other way across.

Mary (*suddenly terrified, drawing back*) I cannot climb that mountain.

Joseph (*starting to climb*) Of course you can. It's like that old woman said. Have faith. Of course it will be hard, tiring. But together . . .

Joseph continues offering silent encouragement as Mary says:

Mary But as Joseph spoke, and as they climbed, Mary felt the world turn around her like a spinning top, faster and faster . . .

The world spins. Mary falls down, grabbing the ground.

Joseph Mary! What is it?

Mary looks up at him, breathless.

Mary I am afraid.

Joseph What of?

Mary I'm too high. I'm going to fall off . . . You can go on without me.

Joseph But you'll die of cold!

Mary Then I'll go home.

Joseph (*coming down*) Mary, come back!

Mary (*to God*) You should never have chosen me! I am not good enough!

The Bush Do not turn back.

Mary Mary had stopped next to an old bush. It was barren, as dead as the mountain itself.

The Bush Or you will never reach your destination.

Mary Who is talking?

The Bush I am a Samaritan. I was cast out by my family and left to die in the mountains. For many years I have lived in this bush. But this is no place for a pregnant woman. You must go on.

Mary I will never get over this mountain!

The Bush (*comfortingly*) Never lose hope. Remember the story that tells us there is always hope.

David appears, aged eight.

Long ago in the town to which you are heading was born a boy called David. Even as a child David was a fighter.

David (*aged eight*) I'll fight anyone! (*He challenges the audience to a fight.*) Come on! Come on then! Fight me! Who's going to fight me? I'm the best fighter in my class. And I can play the harp. But I like fighting best!

The Bush During David's youth, Israel was at war.

The shouts and sounds of war.

A Warrior The enemy was the Philistines. And the Philistines had one fighter greater and more fearsome than any other: Goliath!

Goliath appears. He is colossal, towering over Joseph and Mary.
  Goliath roars and the Israelites scatter in terror. His shadow falls over Mary and Joseph. Goliath laughs and booms his challenge.

Goliath Who will fight me? If any Israelite fights and kills me, then let all Philistines be the servants of Israel! But if I kill them, you Israelites will be our slaves forever!

The Bush No Israelite warrior would dare accept the giant's challenge.

Goliath Will no one fight me?

Various Israelite Warriors Uh, no thanks. Not today. Got an injury.

Goliath (*disappointed*) I want a fight!

Warriors Sorry.

The Bush No one would fight the giant. The Israelites seemed destined to fall under the power of the Philistines for ever. When . . .

David's Voice (*aged thirteen*) I'll fight you!

Goliath What? Did I hear a mouse squeak?

The Bush Goliath tried to see whose voice had spoken. He peered down amongst the Israelites, who desperately struggled to hide the thirteen-year-old David.

Frightened Israelite Warrior I didn't hear anything. Did you hear anything?

Goliath I heard a voice!

Frightened Israelite Warrior No, honest, it must have been a mouse.

Second Israelite Warrior Or a bat.

David (*from under the cloak of an Israelite*) I'll fight anyone!

Goliath There!

Frightened Israelite Warrior A mouse again.

Second Israelite Warrior They're everywhere. It's the heat.

Goliath Who is he who dares to challenge Goliath?

David sneaks from under the skirts of the warriors.

David It is I! David!

He sees Goliath. Goliath sees him.

Ooh.

Goliath Ha ha ha ha. Ha ha ha HA HA HA!

David (*angry at being laughed at*) All right. I'll fight you! You big bully!

Goliath (*wiping tears from his eyes*) Ha ha ha. Oh dear. Oh dear.

David Come on then!

Goliath I'll snap you in two and stir my coffee with your legs and scatter your hair on my soup like pepper!

David Just you try!

David runs between Goliath's legs.

The Bush David ran to the river by his home, and found five smooth stones.

David One, two, three, four, five . . .

The Bush He made a sling from a branch of an old tree and a piece of cloth, and returned to the battleground.

David (*returning*) Let battle commence!

Goliath You're for the crows, boy!

Goliath advances flailing his sword in the air. David ducks and leaps to avoid the swishing blade.

Ha ha ha ha ha! Where are you, fly? I'll kill you for my sport!

But David produces one of his stones and aims the sling at the giant. The stone flies true and straight. It smashes into the forehead of the giant. Goliath stops, shocked.

Oh.

Goliath explodes and crashes to the earth in pieces. David is picked up by the warriors and the trumpets blazon loud.

Warriors David for King!

The Bush And the Philistines were defeated and David became King. That is why they say that hope springs eternal. Because with hope, we are never beaten.

Mary (*looking at the mountain*) I can climb that mountain. (*Lifted by hope, Mary climbs the mountain.*)

Joseph On the twentieth day they approached Jerusalem.
Let's stay in Jerusalem for one night before heading for
Bethlehem. You will be comfortable and we will be fresh
for our final journey.

Mary But the night before, as she slept by the side of the
road, Mary had a dream.

> *A crow flies high in the air, swooping over the
> sleeping Mary before diving down to rip open her
> belly. Mary fights the crow off, screaming.*
> *Joseph, sleeping beside Mary, is woken.*

Joseph Mary! Wake up! Wake up! You are dreaming!

Mary We must not go through Jerusalem. There is evil
there.

Joseph But you need shelter, food.

Mary There is evil there! I saw it in my dream!

Joseph You shouldn't believe your dreams!

Mary A crow swooped and devoured my belly.

Joseph How many more dreams will you have? How
many more angels and devils must you see before we can
reach Bethlehem?

Mary Mary fell silent. Never had Joseph spoken to her
like this. (*to him*) I did not ask for this child. But now it
has happened I celebrate it. I love it. But you may not.
Look at me. If you do not love me, then leave. Go to
Jerusalem. I will continue alone.

> *Joseph debates what to do.*

Donkey The donkey intervened.
May I make a point about love at this juncture?

Joseph What did you say?

184

Donkey Don't look so surprised. Donkeys have opinions too, you know.

Joseph Oh, great.

Donkey Your sad quarrel reminds me of a story my grandfather told me. He had had it told him by his grandfather, who had had it related to him by his mother, who in turn . . .

Mary We get the point.

Donkey Well, it all goes back to a distant donkey ancestor of mine who was an ass in the court of King Solomon!

The donkey leads us into a luscious ancient court. The young King Solomon sits thinking. An Officer runs in.

Officer There is a dispute, my king. Between two women of the night.

Solomon Admit them.

The Officer returns carrying a baby. Two colourfully dressed Prostitutes follow, arguing viciously.

Woman 1 The baby is mine.

Woman 2 He is mine! My lord . . .

Woman 1 My king!

Woman 2 My master!

Woman 1 My liege!

Woman 2 I have been wronged!

Woman 1 I have been abused!

Woman 2 Shamefully wronged!

Woman 1 Disgracefully abused!

Solomon raises his staff. Silence.

Solomon You. Tell your story.

Woman 1 My lord, I am a working woman. I become pregnant. One week ago, I give birth to this beautiful boy. I look in his eyes and see my own. I hold his little head in my hands, and I cry tears of joy. I vow to look after him with all my heart.

Three days later, she also gave birth to a son. But she did not look after him. She put too many covers on him at night and the poor little thing suffocated. So she came in the night while I was sleeping and replaced mine with hers! Now she says mine is the dead baby and this beauty you hold in your hands is hers! (*She breaks down and weeps.*)

Solomon And what do you say to this?

Woman 2 It is true what she says, all of it. Except for one thing. It is I whose baby is alive, and hers who is dead! And it is she who stole my baby that you hold before you!

Woman 1 It is my baby that you hold!

Woman 2 It is my baby!

Donkey As my ancestor tells the story, King Solomon stood and traced a large circle with his staff. No one spoke a word!

Solomon You. Stand on that side. And you on the other.

The women do as ordered. Solomon places the baby in the middle of the circle.

Both of you, take the baby by its arm.

The women approach.

Pull.

Woman 2 What?

Solomon Whoever wants the baby most will win.

Woman 1 Let us start!

Solomon Begin!

Woman 2 No!

Solomon Pull!

Joseph No!

Woman 2 No, let her keep it. It is her child. I was lying. Please. She can take it! Just do not kill it!

The first woman wrenches the baby out of her grasp and holds it aloft like a trophy.

Woman 1 He is mine!

Solomon Now we know who is the mother.

Officer Who?

Donkey Who?

Joseph (*rushing into the scene*) Who? Who?

A pause. Solomon approaches Joseph and hands him the baby.

Solomon You decide. Who loves the child more?

A pause as Joseph thinks. Then he takes the baby and gives it to the second woman.

Joseph Take your son. For you would rather lose your child and see it live than try to keep it and thus see it die. That is true love.

Solomon Now be gone!

And they are. The donkey remains.

Donkey My ancestor tells it like this. Faith sustains us. Hope inspires us. But without love we are nothing. Love is our blood.

Joseph and Mary look at each other.

Joseph We will not go through Jerusalem.

Donkey Good. Onward to Bethlehem! And no more talk of stupid asses!

THREE: THE BIRTH

A gaggle of market traders and lowlifes parade the stage, boasting their wares and their wiles. Card Sharps, Whores, Gamesters, Con Men, Quacks, Traders and Charlatans. Welcome to the market.

Card Sharp Bethlehem was packed with thousands of people arriving to pay the tax.

Trader People with time on their hands and money in their pockets!

Con Man Original star of David! The very one he wore when he killed the giant! One for fifty, two for a pound.

Trader Get your signed picture of Herod here!

Card Sharp Follow the queen and double your money!

Whore Follow this queen and you won't care about money!

Quack Diseases, plagues and afflictions cured in an instant! Witness the blind seeing and the lame walking.

An obviously planted blind man rises.

Blind Man I can see. Oh, you worker of miracles, you healer of the damned!

Quack This could be you, ladies and gentlemen!

Spice Seller Take this spice every morning and live for ever!

Crystal Ball Seller Learn your fortune! See into the mists of the future and all will become clear!

Palmist Have your hand read! If you don't like what you hear, have the other read for half-price!

Joseph Joseph and Mary entered the city at dusk.

People bustle past Joseph and Mary.

Mary Mary was knocked from side to side by the throngs of people buying and selling, drinking, fighting, yelling and screaming.

Joseph They fought their way through the teeming crowds until they reached the centre.
We must find somewhere to stay.

The traders and hawkers rush over to ensnare them.

Traders Stars of David! Small Noah's arks! Buy two replica ten commandments tablets and I'll throw in a Moses basket for free!

Joseph Let us through!

Quack Make way! I'm a doctor. This woman needs my help!

Palmist Let me read your palm for the child! You must be a very proud father! This way for a reading!

Joseph and Mary are physically separated by the traders.

Mary Joseph!

Joseph Mary! Where are you?

Spice Seller Take this spice for eternal life!

Trader Get your signed picture of Herod here!

Card Sharp Follow the queen and double your money!

Joseph Let me go!

Crystal Ball Seller I can see the baby in my ball. It's a girl! A beautiful bright-faced girl. A silver coin and I'll tell you more!

Mary Joseph!

Joseph Let go of me! Mary!

They are lifted in the air and valiantly fight their way back together. Mary hugs Joseph tight.

Mary I lost you.

Joseph Here I am.

The traders circle the couple, menacingly whispering their offers and sales.

We're not buying anything. We just want somewhere to stay for the night!

Sellers You won't find a room now. Not at this time. The place is packed. Look around you! Ha ha ha. Ha ha ha.

They look around. 'No Vacancy' signs meet them wherever they go.

Mary We must find a room!

An Old Man I have a room.

Joseph An old man stood before them. His head was shaped like an egg. His face was pale, as if he had not seen the sun in centuries.

Mary Where is it?

Old Man Not far from here. In the middle of town.

Joseph What kind of room?

Old Man The best. A large bed of red velvet. Covers of the purest silk. Pillows of feathers from African swans. Carpets woven from the wool of the Eastern lands. Curtains of fine lace spun by ancient hands.

Joseph (*awestruck*) How much is it?

Old Man Normally I charge two gold coins per night.

Joseph Two gold coins!

Old Man And it should by rights be more. It's very busy at the moment, everyone is here for the tax. It's the loveliest room in my house, and my house is the finest house in the whole town.

Joseph and Mary We have nothing like this money!

Old Man But seeing as the lady is expecting . . . you shall have it for nothing.

Mary and Joseph Oh, thank you. Thank you. Please take us there!

Joseph They tried to kiss the old man's hand.

Mary But he drew back in disgust.

Old Man We have no time for this frivolity! Come with me!

They start to walk.

Joseph They followed the old man. But soon they saw they were starting to leave the centre.

I thought you said your house was in the centre of the town.

Old Man My house is in the new centre. It is superior to the old centre.

Mary Suddenly the baby kicked in Mary's stomach. It was like a warning.

Who is this man?

Now shadowy figures join the Old Man. Now another. Now two more. And another two.

Joseph Who are these men?

Old Man My sons.

Mary Why do they all limp?

Old Man It is a flaw in the family.

Joseph Further and further they walked into the darkest part of the town. No lights came from the windows of the houses. Silence surrounded them.

The men light flame torches as the darkness descends.

Please. It is getting dark. Take us back. Take us back to the centre.

Old Man No rooms in the centre.

Mary You said you lived in the centre. You liar!

The men turn. Dark shadows in the street.

Man You come with us.

Another Man There is no way back.

Another Man And we are almost there.

The Men Look.

Joseph They looked and saw a small dark house in the darkest corner of the street.

Mary It was black as coal, as if it had suffered a great fire and yet not fallen. The windows were boarded up. The doorway hung open.

Joseph I thought you said yours was the finest house in the town.

Old Man Wait until you see inside . . . Come.

They enter the house.

Joseph They entered and were greeted by a spiral staircase leading down for as far as they could see. The air smelt of smoke and burning flesh.

Old Man Come.

Joseph Where are the carpets from the Eastern lands?

Old Man It is all waiting for you. Come.

Mary The baby kicked again. What does it mean?

Joseph Down they went, further and further, until they reached a small windowless room. It was hotter than the desert sun.

Mary Inside there was nothing.

Joseph No bed.

Mary No curtains.

Joseph No window.

Mary No light. Nothing.
You said this was the loveliest room in your house!

Joseph You promised us pillows of swan's feathers, and curtains of the finest silk!

Old Man And you shall have them. You shall have it all, my friends, everything that you desire!
  But first you must give me what I want.

Joseph I'm not giving you two gold coins for this room!

Old Man I don't want two gold coins.

Joseph Then what do you want?

  The old man stops dead and points to Mary's belly.

Old Man I want him.

Mary And Mary heard a small voice inside her, as if it was the voice of the child itself, saying, 'This man is the devil, and this place is called hell.'

  Mary and Joseph look at each other.

Old Man Give me the child and I will make you richer and more powerful than Herod himself.
  Refuse, and I will tear the child from your belly and leave you here to rot for eternity.

  They look around. The men stare intently at Mary's belly. A drumming begins.

Mary I will never give birth here.

Old Man I'll give you everything! The earth will be your garden! Just give me the child!

Mary Never!

Old Man Give me the child or die!

Joseph Never!

Old Man Then I must take him from you.

  The men don cloaks and masks, macabre versions of operating-theatre costume.

Mary and Joseph stand in horror. The men circle the pregnant woman.

Joseph Mary, run!

Mary No, wait! Have faith, Joseph.

The men bring out operating instruments. They stamp the ground with their feet and circle closer. Then suddenly they take hold of Mary. An operating table appears and they lay her on it.

Mary Have faith, Joseph!

The men hold their knives and scalpels above Mary and chant.

Believe!

Joseph I believe!

The men make to bring down their knives upon Mary's belly.
A great screaming is heard. It is from the devils themselves, as they see, to their horror, that Mary has disappeared.

Old Man (*in a rage of horror*) Where is she? Where is she? Find her! Kill her!

Joseph But when they started to look for Mary, they all saw her face in each others'.

The Men She is here! No, she is here! No, she is here!

Joseph And in their rage they started to attack each other!

They attack each other, chopping limbs and heads off, until nothing exists of any of them but their black, smoking cloaks.

The Men Aaaaaaaah!

*The screams of the men in an eternity of torture fade
into the dark night . . .*

Joseph (*standing alone*) Mary? Mary, where are you?
Mary!!

Mary Hello, Joseph.

Mary appears unharmed.

Joseph But I saw them, with the knives . . . They were . . .
Where are they? Where are we?
  They were back on the street. The night was quiet and
still. And of the devil's hotel, there was no sign. It was as
if it had never existed.

Mary Suddenly they heard singing.

A fat Innkeeper enters drunkenly. He sings.

Innkeeper
  My inn is full
  My belly is full
  My pockets are full
  Ah, life is wonderful!

He belches a huge belch.

My inn hasn't been as full as this since the weekend after
the earth tremor. And that day I forgot to charge anyone!
Well, not this time! Who said I was too soft to make
money! Ha! I've made a fortune! Soft Ezra indeed.
Crafty schemer Ezra more like. Money-grabbing-old-fox
Ezra the innkeeper. Cunning-as-a-panther Ezra. Grrrr.
Grrr.
  Ah, the night sky looks so beautiful when you've just
made a fortune! Each star like a small coin. And the
moon a big silver one! Ha ha ha. Everything's beautiful.
Even my wife looks beautiful tonight. I might even sleep
in the same bed as her. I might. (*He belches again.*) I'm

charging double the normal rate. Per person. One room's got twenty people in! If I wasn't so happy I'd have to feel a bit guilty. Guilty? Panther-fox Ezra feeling guilt? Don't know the meaning of the word.

Oh yes, tonight's a night to get drunk and celebrate one's winnings. Tonight, Ezra the innkeeper, drunken Ezra, fat sow Ezra, is a winner! A winner!

Come on, let's count the money again. I know how much there is but it's such fun! (*He takes out his bag of coins and lays them on the floor.*) One, two, three, four, five . . .

Mary Excuse me?

Innkeeper Sorry, we're completely full and anyway I doubt you could afford my exorbitant rates. Six, seven, eight . . .

Mary Excuse me.

Innkeeper Now look what you've done. I have to start again now.

Mary What are you doing?

Innkeeper I'm counting the money that I have so ruthlessly procured from ordinary people.

Joseph So we heard.

Innkeeper Yes, there's no denying it. I'm a bad man. A rough sort. You can trust me as far as you can throw me. Which isn't far. You know the type. No human feelings at all. Not a sensitive bone in my body. Money money money. That's my sole concern. (*He looks closer.*) Oh my God, you're pregnant. Oh, you poor girl. What are you doing out on a night like this?

Mary We've been trying to find a place to stay.

Innkeeper Oh that's terrible. And you look so tired. When's it due?

Mary Any time now.

Innkeeper Oh that's wonderful. My wife and I, we have two boys and a girl. They're so lovely. The day my daughter was born was the happiest day of my life. Her little fat face . . . (*He weeps.*) She was so beautiful and chubby . . . the midwife said she'd never seen bigger. You'll make good parents, I can see you will. Can I touch it?

Mary If you like.

Innkeeper touches it.

Innkeeper Oh yes, beautiful, beautiful baby. Very round. It's a good sign. Now, where was I?

Joseph You were counting your money.

Innkeeper Oh, that can wait. Childbirth – it's a miracle, it really is. So you poor people, you have nowhere to stay . . . Let me think . . . let me think . . . I must be able to help . . .

The Innkeeper does some exaggerated thinking and walking around.
What he doesn't notice is that a thief has seen his money and is approaching it. The thief takes the money and runs into the night.

Joseph Your money!

Innkeeper What money? Oh, that money. (*He turns to see it gone.*) My money! My money! Where did it go? My money went away! Oh, I'm such a fool! (*He hits himself repeatedly.*) What will my wife say? She's not one to annoy, Mrs Ezra. Woe is me. Woe!

Mary approaches him.

Mary You were only trying to help us.

Innkeeper Yes, but I wanted to be hard of heart and quick of cunning. Like a panther! Grrrr. Oh, it's no good. I'm not a panther. I'm just a soft moggy! Miaow. Miaow. (*He brushes his head against Mary like a domestic cat.*)

Mary What were you going to say?

Innkeeper That I'm a fat puss!

Mary No, what were you going to say to us?

Innkeeper Hmmn? Oh, just that you could stay in the stable if you like. It's round the back. It's not much, but at least it's covered and I can find some clean straw.

Mary That would be wonderful.

Innkeeper You wouldn't have to pay. I've made so much money tonight anyway.

Pause.

Oh no. I haven't! I haven't! (*He hits himself again.*) Still, you won't pay. Pussycat Ezra is a man of his word. Oh, I shall receive a prize beating for this.

Mary suddenly feels a crumpling pain.

Yes, something like that. Oh, what?

Joseph What is it?

Mary I think it's happening . . . (*She smiles.*)

Innkeeper Oh. Oh. Um. Oh.

Joseph Where is the stable?

Innkeeper Stable?

Joseph The stable!

Innkeeper Oh, *the* stable! I've forgotten.

Mary You said it's round the back.

Innkeeper Yes! It's round the back. Oh my!

Joseph They hurried around the back of the inn. There was a stable, packed with sheep, horses and donkeys.

They go round the back. Some straw falls. It is by no means clean. Animals graze in the stable. Horses. Donkeys.

You mean here?

Innkeeper It's all I've got! Sorry about the smell. Here's some straw. And a blanket.

Joseph It's mouldy.

Innkeeper It's all I've got!

Mary feels another pain.

Mary It's beginning.

Innkeeper Lie down.

Mary I want to sit.

Joseph Have you a milking stool?

Innkeeper Only a bar stool.

Joseph Fetch it. And a saw.

Innkeeper Yes!

He does. Joseph expertly turns it into a birth stool. Mary watches. The animals also. As he works, they start to make noise, a chorus of animal sounds.
    Mary sits.

Mary It is happening!

*Animal music. The animals bay and stamp the ground.
The Innkeeper cries and busies himself, running in
circles. Joseph pours water on Mary's head.*

It is happening!

Innkeeper For eight hours she screamed the same words!

Mary It is happening!

Innkeeper The animals bayed and her husband wiped
her face and spoke to her in a soft voice. I fetched water
and food for him and watched this amazing sight!

Mary (*exhausted*) It is happening!

Innkeeper Then suddenly, a remarkable event! The noises
of the town dimmed and became silent. The lights of the
town flickered and extinguished! The world slowed, and
time itself stretched into an eternity! The father fell to
the earth and prostrated himself. The mother gazed
heavenwards. And a light like a river of white fire
poured from the sky into her belly. And I, poor dumb
oaf of an innkeeper, fell and worshipped in pure wonder!

*The animal music reaches a climax. Then suddenly:
silence and stillness. A bright light shines from Mary's
belly.
    The Innkeeper prostrates himself.
    Mary stares around her in exhausted awe and
wonder.*

Mary The world is silent. The world is still. It does not
turn. It waits for you.
    Be born, child.

*The torches above the stable blow out. Darkness.
    End of Act One.*

Act Two

PROLOGUE

Herod asleep in his royal bed. A storm outside. The linen sheets and silken covers stifle him as he turns and tosses in turbulent dreams . . .

An Attendant That night, King Herod was sleeping in his royal bed . . .

An Attendant In his royal chamber . . .

Another Attendant In his royal palace in Jerusalem . . .

Attendant When a storm broke and Herod was besieged by a terrible dream.

> *The white sheets rise and stifle Herod as he tosses in sleeping agony.*

Herod Aaaaaahhhhhh! Help me! Help me!

Attendants My lord!

> *They rush to help him. Herod wakes.*

Herod Aaaaah! . . . What? Where am I?

Attendants In your chamber, your majesty.
Wake up, your majesty.

Minister of Justice You were dreaming, my lord.

King Herod I dreamt the land was washed away by an ocean of pure white light. I was drowning, drowning deeper and deeper into darkness . . . I saw a face, the pale face of a child. But I couldn't touch it. A dark cloud came between us. It is an omen. Something is happening . . .

Minister of Justice! Awaken my spies. Find out if a child has been born this night. Wherever it is . . . it must be destroyed!

ONE: BENJAMIN THE SHEPHERD

The crack of thunder, the howling of wind, and the pouring of rain. A hill above Bethlehem. A group of sheep grazing. A huddle of poor clown Shepherds shelter under oilskins from the wind and the rain.

Shepherd 1 That night, on a hill above Bethlehem, three poor shepherds were tending their master's sheep.

Shepherd 3 Is it still raining?

Shepherd 2 looks up and is soaked with water.

Shepherd 2 Yup.

Shepherd 3 All our sheep still there?

Shepherds 1 and 2 count the audience.

All still there.

Shepherd 1 (*looking closer at audience*) Ugly bounders aren't they, sheep?

Shepherd 2 But maybe under that woolly exterior they're thinking great thoughts. (*looking closer*) And then again maybe they're not.

Shepherd 3 Weather still not clearing up?

Shepherd 1 looks up. He is soaked too.

Shepherd 1 Nope.

Shepherd 3 That's strange. Twenty minutes ago everything was still as a pond in summer, and now mayhem and chaos.

Shepherd 1 And everyone safe in their homes except for us.

Shepherd 2 Except us.

The howling of a mad animal in the darkness. The Shepherds poke their heads out in fright. They are all immediately soaked. The howling starts again.

What was that?

The howling begins again. The Shepherds tumble from their oilskins in fear. The Third Shepherd crosses himself.

Shepherd 1 What is it?

Shepherd 3 It's the beast of the hills.

Shepherd 2 The what?

Shepherd 3 Do you not know the legend of the mad beast that roams the hills at night, killing sheep and eating shepherds alive?

Shepherd 2 No. I didn't know that legend. Did you know about that?

Shepherd 1 No. I hadn't heard about that.

Shepherds 1 and 2 Aaah!

They panic. But Shepherd 3 calms them.

Shepherd 3 Stay calm. The beast only attacks those that move or shake with fear.

The Shepherds move and shake with fear.

Shepherd 1 You're shaking!

Shepherd 2 I'm not shaking. He's shaking!

Shepherd 3 I'm not shaking! He's shaking!

And so on until . . .

Shepherd 3 Sssshhh!

The howling comes suddenly nearer.
   They back away from the sound and bump into
each other, causing much terror.

Shepherds Aaaaah! Shhhhh!

Shepherd 3 Wait! I've got an idea!

Shepherds 1 and 2 What?

Shepherd 3 We'll hide!

Shepherds 1 and 2 Brilliant!

They try to hide, but there is nothing to hide behind.
They hide behind each other, but it's no good. Now
the howling is quite close. They moan.

Shepherd 3 Wait! I've got an idea.

Shepherds 1 and 2 What?

Shepherd 3 We'll talk to it!

Shepherds 1 and 2 Brilliant! You go first. No, you go
first.

Shepherd 1 Now listen here, beast. You come near our
sheep, we'll kill you with our bare hands!

The beast howls. Shepherd 1 leaps into the arms of
Shepherd 2.

Shepherd 2 Any other brilliant ideas?

Evidently not.

We're going to die.

A mad creature appears, howling.

Shepherd 1 Aaaaah!

Shepherd 2 Aaaaah!

Shepherd 3 Aaaaaah!

They run around in circles. The beast runs around after them. They run away so fast that they end up catching it up by accident and trapping it underneath them.

Shepherd 1 Where is it?

Shepherd 2 Where is it?

Shepherd 3 Where is it?

They feel underneath them.

We've captured the beast of the hills!

Shepherds 1 and 2 We've captured the beast of the hills! Ha ha!

Shepherd 2 We'll be heroes! Ha ha!

Shepherd 1 Quick! Kill it!

Shepherd 2 How?

Shepherd 3 Cut off its head!

Shepherds 1 and 2 Ah ha!

They expose the head of the creature ready to chop it off. It is a man in his early thirties, with a foolish grin and a tragic clown's eyes. It is Benjamin the Shepherd.

Benjamin Baaaooooooow!

Shepherds It's Benjamin the Mad Shepherd!

They cuff him.

Shepherd 2 Benjamin! We thought we'd caught the beast of the hills!

Benjamin I am the beast! Baoooow!

Shepherd 1 I'll teach you to pretend to be a beast! In my house, beasts get the stick taken to them!

> *He begins to beat Benjamin with his crook. Benjamin leaps around the stage, howling.*

Shepherd 3 Leave him now. He's soft in the head, poor fellow. He knows no better.

Benjamin Baaaoooow! I am the beast and I will gobble your children!

Shepherd 2 Yes, we're really scared, Benjamin.

Benjamin I will enter your cottage while you are asleep and eat them all up.

Shepherd 3 Leave him. Mad, he is.

Shepherd 1 There's not one madder. Even his sheep's mad. Look.

> *One scruffy lunatic sheep enters, baaaing insanely. Benjamin runs to embrace it.*

Benjamin My child, my little child.

Shepherd 1 Only got one left. All the rest have died of hunger.

Shepherd 3 I challenge you to find a disease that sheep hasn't got.

Benjamin (*hugging the sheep*) Babe, sweet babe, where did you go?
And your mother so fair, dead of grief.

Shepherd 1 What's he saying?

Shepherd 3 Poor man. It's his wife and child he's ranting about.

Shepherd 2 Benjamin has a wife and child?

Shepherd 3 He did have.

Benjamin Biaoooow! Biaoooow!

Shepherd 3 Benjamin was the finest shepherd in the land. He had the most beautiful wife and the sweetest child you ever could see. Then one day the child was killed by a mad dog on the road. His wife died of grief. And Benjamin started to live like a wild animal. Now he lives nowhere, drinks from puddles, and keeps company only with the trees and the wind.

> *Shepherd 2 starts to cry and is consoled.*
> *Benjamin wrestles himself on the ground.*

Benjamin Baaaooow! (*He leaps up and approaches a sheep.*)

Sheep Baaaa.

Benjamin King Herod! Your majesty, I kiss your feet.

Shepherd 2 It's a sheep you're talking to, Benjamin.

Benjamin King Herod, may I wash your royal feet in the waters of the royal fountain? (*He pisses on the sheep.*) What's that you say, King Herod? You want me to be your prime minister? I thank you, your royal highness. Baaa. (*Benjamin kisses the sheep and becomes a sheep prime minister, baaing importantly.*)

Shepherd 3 Calm now, Benjamin.

Benjamin (*seeing them*) Good evening, gentlemen. I have been appointed prime minister to the great King Herod. Baaa.

Shepherd 1 You know who we are, Benjamin?

Benjamin Of course. (*to Shepherd 1*) You are my home baaa secretary, you are my foreign baaa secretary and you are my chancellor baaa of the exchequer. Together we rule the land! Home baaa secretary, how are things proceeding?

Shepherd 3 Play along with him, poor fellow.

Shepherd 2 Home baaa affairs are going very well, thank you.

Benjamin Excellent. And what news from you, chancellor?

Shepherd 1 Only good news.

Benjamin Excellent! Are we baaa taxing enough? I want lots of baaa taxes. For example, are we baaa taxing people who walk like this? (*He walks madly.*)

Shepherds Yes yes, we are.

Benjamin Excellent! (*Benjamin suddenly spies something. He runs over and stares madly at a member of the audience. Then he runs over to the Shepherds.*) You know who that is, don't you?

Shepherd 1 It's a sheep, Benjamin.

Benjamin You naive fool. That is a spy. In disguise. He/She's spying on our cabinet meeting, trying to assassinate me. We must arrest him/her immediately.

Benjamin approaches the member of the audience, smiles at him/her falsely, then leaps on him/her. The other Shepherds pull him off.

Shepherds Leave him/her alone!

Benjamin (*furious*) He/she's a spy!

Shepherd 3 (*clipping him*) That's enough of your visions now, Benjamin! Enough!

Benjamin (*suddenly cowed*) Biaaaow! Biaaaow!

Shepherd 2 Go to bed, Benjamin!

The thunder cracks. Benjamin howls.

Shepherds Go to bed, mad shepherd! You and your crazy visions!

They retire under their oilskins.
  Alone, Benjamin approaches the lunatic sheep sadly.

Benjamin Bed time, little girl.

Sheep Baaaa. Baaaa.

Benjamin hugs the sheep and is about to lie down when he suddenly sees a star.

Benjamin A star!

The star moves across the sky.

It's moving. It's moving! Wake up! The star's moving! Wake up, wake up! The star is moving!

The Shepherds tumble out of their oilskins.

Shepherds What star? What star is moving?

Benjamin There! There!

But it is gone.

Shepherd 3 There'll be no stars in this weather, Benjamin. Go to bed now.

Benjamin I saw it. It moved across the sky . . .

Shepherds You're seeing things.

Benjamin It was there, I swear!

Shepherds Go to bed, Benjamin! Before we get angry. A star that moves! Whatever next?

Benjamin But . . .

The shepherds go back to bed. Benjamin scratches his head.

I'm sure I saw it.

The star appears, but Benjamin does not see it at first.

Or am I mad? Dear God, tell me which it is! (*He looks heavenwards and sees the star.*) The star. The star!

The star moves across the sky.

The star is moving! The star is moving! Wake up! Wake up!

He wakes the other Shepherds.

Shepherds What now?

Benjamin The star is there! It's moving!

He points to where it was. But it is no longer there. The Shepherds turn on him.

Shepherds You idiot! You try this again, we'll be forced to beat you.

Benjamin But there was a star.

Shepherds There was no star!

Benjamin There was! It moved!

Shepherds There was no star! Say it! There was no star!

Benjamin There was!

They advance on him. He leaps back in fright.

No star! No star!

Shepherds Good. Now get some sleep, and don't interrupt us again.

They return under their covers. Benjamin looks around.

Benjamin There was no star! There was no star, you fool! You idiot! Star indeed! Now I know. I am mad. If I look up I will see it again, because I am mad, and I will receive a beating. I must look down so as not to see it! (*He throws himself to the ground and buries his face in the earth.*) I will not lift my head until day breaks! Don't look up! Don't look up.

The star appears again. Benjamin remains face down. The sheep sees the star.

Sheep Baaaaa.

Benjamin Quiet, my child. I can't come to you now. I must bury my eyes in the ground so I cannot see.

Sheep Baaaaa. Baaaaa.

Benjamin Oh please be quiet. I cannot come to you.

Sheep Baaaaa. Baaaa. Baaaa. Staaaa. Staaaa. Staaar! Staaar!

Benjamin lifts his head in amazement. Is the sheep really saying 'Staaaar'?
  Petrified he looks up at the star. It moves across the sky.

Sheep Staaar!

Sheep and Benjamin Staaar! Staaaar! Staaar! STAAAR!

The other Shepherds are woken and leap up.

Shepherds That's it! You've had your warning! You're going to be given a beating you won't forget!

Sheep Staaar.

The Shepherds stop in shock.

Shepherd 1 Did that sheep just talk?

Sheep Staaar!

Shepherd 2 Whooooh!

Sheep STAAAR!

They look up. The star moves across the sky.

Shepherds Staaaar!! Staaaar!!

Shepherd 1 It moves! What do we do?

Shepherds Benjamin. What do we do?

Sheep Follow.

Benjamin Follow!

Shepherds Follow!

The Shepherds leap up and run after the star.

All Follow!

Shepherds They ran like madmen across fields and over hills, following the bright star in the sky.

Benjamin Benjamin ran ahead and was first to reach the sleeping town. The star came to rest over the stable of a small inn. And there, there . . .

The Angel Gabriel, in beggar form, greets Benjamin.

Who are you?

Gabriel I am the Angel Gabriel.

Benjamin Hello, I'm Benjamin.

Gabriel Benjamin. Ten years ago this night, you lost a child and became mad. Now you will find a new child, and become sane. Because you believed where others had only doubt, you will be first. Come . . .

Benjamin weeps sweet tears of joy and is about to enter when . . .

213

TWO: THE WISE MEN

Enter Herod and his spies.

Herod In Jerusalem, Herod's spies had been trying to discover something that could explain his horrible dream.

Spy 1 I have searched every town in the region, your majesty. There is nothing to report.

Herod Nothing?

Spy 1 Just a bunch of shepherds in Bethlehem yelling about a moving star.

Minister of Justice Don't pay attention to that rabble of lowlifes. They were probably drunk.

Herod Then how can my dream be explained? I must know! All of you, go from my sight and don't come back until you have found what it is that is haunting me!

Spy 2 (*rushes in*) My lord. Three men have arrived in the city. Their feet are bare and all they have for clothes are shirts covered in dirt and holes. They wish to see you.

Herod See me? Worthless tramps. Banish them immediately.

Spy 2 My lord. They claim to be kings from the East.

Herod Kings in rags? What devilish games are being played on me this night?

Minister of Justice They are doubtless confidence tricksters, my lord. I will imprison them forthwith.

Herod Excellent! But how can I be sure?!
  Bring them before me!

Pause. Enter three men in nightshirts, soiled and exhausted. Herod laughs.

So you are kings from the East, are you?

The entire court laughs contemptuously.

Caspar Not just kings. We are the richest men in the world!

An exotic gong crashes and the kings bow, as Herod watches in horror.

Caspar!

Melchior Melchior!

Balthazar And Balthazar!

Herod Not Balthazar, Caspar and Melchior of Ecbatana?

Balthazar The very same.

Herod But Caspar's mile-long stables of pure Arabian white horses are legendary.
And who has not heard of Melchior's thousand carriages of crusted jewels and rare silks?
And who has not spoken in hushed tones of the white marble palaces of Balthazar?
So what happened? Were you thrown out by murderous revolutionaries, poisoned by your wives, or overthrown by jealous subjects?

Caspar Nothing of the kind.
We all rule over dominions of beauty and plenitude.

Melchior We all have wives of beauty, and children of distinction.

Balthazar And we are all respected as equal in wisdom as in wealth.

Herod So what went wrong!

Melchior We were all bored.

Herod Bored!?

Balthazar Bored.

Caspar Utterly and totally bored.

Melchior Whether playing quoits with diamonds . . .

Caspar Or riding stallions through our infinite lands . . .

Balthazar Or bathing in the pearl-encrusted tubs filled to the brim with yaks' milk . . .

Kings Or dining on rare meats and exotic sweets that melted in the mouth. Or ministering to a thousand subjects. Or watching plays and entertainments. Or drinking fine wines. Or being massaged by oils from antique lands. Or or or . . .

Balthazar Life was without meaning.

Melchior And without meaning, life isn't worth living.

Caspar We had only one delight: to meet once a year to compare notes on the night sky.

Balthazar To discuss findings . . .

Melchior And to receive prophecy in the stars.

Herod The stars. What about the stars?

Caspar We had agreed to meet this year in the court of Melchior.

The court.

Balthazar On arrival, we sent away our myriad servants.
Tonight we do not need you.
And proceeded together . . .

216

Melchior To the vast oak planetarium in the heart of Melchior's palace . . .

Caspar To study the night sky.

The night sky lights up.

The Three Alone at last! No servants! No concubines!

Balthazar Just us and the heavens. This is paradise!

They stare at it in anticipation.

Caspar We waited.

Time passes, literally.

Balthazar We waited.

Time passes again.

Melchior And waited.

Time passes again.

Caspar Nothing happened.

Herod Ha! All fable and fiction!

Melchior Never had the night sky been so dull.

Caspar I have to return to my massive kingdom. Oh misery.

Balthazar I must travel back to my hundred wives. Oh despair.

Melchior Another year of luxurious tedium.
But as we left, we saw that we had not blown out the candle.

Herod Of course not. You have myriad servants for that sort of thing.

Caspar But we've sent them all to bed so we can be alone with the stars.

217

Herod So wake one up!

Balthazar (*excited*) I've never blown a candle out before.

Caspar It might be enjoyable.

Herod Nonsense!

Melchior But we all want to.

Herod But you are masters of a million subjects! You can't blow out your own candle!

Caspar But we did. All three of us.

They blow as one. And immediately a wonderful star appears in the night sky. Darkness below. Heavenly music.

Herod What is that?

Caspar The star that will lead us to a holy child!

Herod (*horrified*) A child. What child?

Herod stares in horror as the star begins to move.

It moves!

Balthazar It headed west.

Caspar We abandoned our kingdoms . . .

Melchior And pursued it like men possessed across the desert!

Balthazar We took with us gifts for the child!

Caspar I brought forty carriages of gold.

Balthazar And I great vats of frankincense.

Melchior And I several tonnes of myrrh.
We will bow down before this holy king. And life will have meaning!

*Men, camels and carriages flood the stage. The
journey begins.*

Caspar On the journey, disaster befell us!

Balthazar First, ten of our carriages were sent flying over
a rock edge and tumbling into an abyss.

Melchior Then, hundreds of servants died of disease.

Caspar Eighty more carriages were lost in a flooded
river, taking several hundred servants with them.

Balthazar The rest of the servants fled into the
mountains, fearing that the expedition was damned.

Melchior We were alone!

Caspar On our first night, as we slept, our food was
stolen by animals.

Balthazar Then we were robbed by brigands, who took
the carriage containing the gifts! We had nothing!

Herod So you turned back!

Caspar Back to meaningless luxury?

Melchior Back to abominable money?

Balthazar Back to sterile power? No, we went on!
And as we walked naked through the desert, a bird flew
over . . .

Melchior And dropped gifts from the sky!

Caspar Into my hand fell a nugget of gold!

Balthazar Into mine a small vial of frankincense.

Melchior And into mine a little pot of myrrh.

Herod But where did they come from?

Balthazar Don't you understand? It was the child's work!

Melchior Suddenly, we felt this soaring happiness envelop us!

Balthazar And we continued on our journey, accompanied only by a wonderful feeling . . .

Caspar Of joy!

Herod A star that moves?! A bird dropping gifts! A child! A child!! What is happening to my mind?

Minister of Justice My lord, these men are clearly insane.

Balthazar The star will lead us to a child. A child that will grow to be the holiest of kings!

Melchior We want to bow down before him and offer him our gifts.

Caspar He is nearby. But we don't know where. Can you help us?

Herod (*suddenly charming*) With pleasure.
  Herod dismissed the kings and summoned his high priests!
  A child has been born this last night. He is destined to be the holiest and mightiest of kings. Holier and mightier than me. I need to know exactly where he is.

Priests The priests studied their holy books. And returned to Herod.
  He will be born in Bethlehem. As it is prophesied in the holy book: 'From Bethlehem shall come a ruler who will govern my people Israel.'

Herod NEVER! NEVER!
  A plan sprouted in the mind of Herod.
  Kings of the East, I hear you wish to worship this new King?

Kings We do.

Herod Then know, it is spoken by the prophecy that you will find him in Bethlehem.

Go. And when you have found him, return immediately and tell me where he lies. I also wish to worship this child. For he will rule over Israel.

Kings Yes, my lord.

They leave.

Herod NEVER!!

Caspar The kings set off for Bethlehem without delay.

Balthazar As night came on, the sky cleared.

Melchior And there was the star once more!

Caspar It came to rest over a tiny dirty stable behind an old ill-kept inn.

Balthazar And there . . .

Caspar There . . .

Melchior There . . .

The scene of the nativity is suddenly revealed. Mary, Joseph and the child attended by Benjamin the Shepherd, Ezra the Innkeeper and animals.
The kings, whose dress is noticeably similar to that of Benjamin, bow down in adoration.

Mary You lost everything. Now you have found everything.

Balthazar Never had the kings felt such happiness.

Caspar This is the child we sought.

Melchior It is a miracle!

THREE: THE MASSACRE OF THE INNOCENTS

Caspar That night the kings slept by the mother and baby's side. Although the ground was hard and they had no coverings to protect them from the cold, it was the deepest sleep they had ever slept.

Melchior Their intention was to leave for Jerusalem in the morning to tell King Herod where he could find the child so he too could come to worship him.

Balthazar But that night, as they slept, all had the same ominous dream.

> *A crow flies high in the air, swooping over the sleeping Mary and child.*
> *Now hundreds of crows fill the air in a cacophony of vile screaming.*
> *The crows dive down to attack the child. The kings wake up and fight the crows off, screaming.*

Balthazar Take that!

Caspar Get away from here!

Melchior Away from this wondrous child!

> *The crows disappear. The men are left flailing in thin air. Mary and Joseph wake.*

Mary Gentlemen. Wake up.

Balthazar (*waking*) The crows! Where are the crows!

Melchior They were attacking the child!

Mary You were dreaming.

Caspar Dreaming?

Balthazar We dreamt of crows attacking the child.

Melchior What can it mean?

Joseph Joseph remembered Mary's dream when the crow attacked her pregnant belly with its claws.

Kings When did you dream this?

Mary As we approached Jerusalem.

Kings Jerusalem!?

Mary What is it?

Caspar They told the mother and father what had happened in Jerusalem.

Balthazar Of their conversation with Herod and the prophecy of the high priests.

Melchior And how they were due to return there to tell him of the child so he too could come and worship.

Joseph Do not go to him. He is the crow of whom you dreamed. Return home by another route as we came here by another route.

Kings The kings agreed. And avoiding the city of Jerusalem they began the long journey back to their homes.

Mary So, husband, you believe in dreams after all . . .

Herod's palace.

Attendant Herod's palace! The kings were due to return with their news!

Herod The day went by like a slow river. Herod grew angry. Where are those kings? I ordered them to return immediately to me with news of the child.

Minister of Justice It is possible they did not find this child.

Herod You don't believe this child exists, do you?

Minister of Justice My lord. It does seem very unlikely.

Herod Maybe you are right. Moving stars. Birds carrying gifts. Omens! Dreams! All nonsense!
   And he laughed a wild hollow cackle of a laugh that was heard through all the corridors of the palace.
   Ha ha ha. HA HA HA.

Spy His laugh was interrupted by a spy.
   My lord, the three kings from the East have been spied escaping through a remote province back to their own lands.

Herod They have betrayed me! The child does exist! I can feel it. Remember the prophecy: born to rule over my people Israel! I have been tricked!
   (*turning on Minister of Justice*) Who was it who told me to ignore the prophecy? Who laughed at the idea of a moving star, and of kings in rags?

Minister of Justice My lord, please . . .

Herod It was you! You traitor. You would have me ignore these signs so you can take my place! Guards, seize this man! Arrest him, try him fairly, torture and execute him.

Minister of Justice My lord!

Herod Away with him!

   The Minister of Justice is seized and taken away screaming.

What do I do now? What do I do?
   This child is born to rule over Israel. I could go to worship him, as the kings of the East did. Bow down to one greater than I.

Me worship a child! Impossible! Who is king? Who rules this land!

(*to the spy*) You. Call the commander of my soldiers.

Commander My lord.

Herod You are faithful to me, are you not?

Commander My lord.

Herod Willing to fulfil my every command.

Commander Yes, my lord.

Herod Then listen. There is a child born this last day in Bethlehem. This child is dangerous. He must not live.

Commander Yes, my lord.

Herod Wait. I do not know the exact location of the child.

Commander My lord?

Herod I know he is in Bethlehem, but not where. Tonight you will enter Bethlehem with a thousand men armed with swords and sabres. You will knock on the door of every house and inn. And you will kill the firstborn of every family. Only then will I know that he is dead.

Commander My lord, there are several thousand people in Bethlehem.

Herod And? Why do you flinch?

Commander But my lord . . .

Herod Did you not vow to be faithful to me in all things?

Commander Yes, my lord.

Herod To fulfil my every command!

Commander Yes, my lord . . .

Herod And now you question me . . .

Commander But my lord . . .

Herod Yes! Your lord! I am your lord! No one but me is your lord!
  Do as I desire. Or pay the consequences.

Commander The commander gathered his forces and gave them their orders.
  You are to march on Bethlehem. You are to knock on every door. You are to search every house and inn. And you are to kill every new-born baby.
  As night fell, the soldiers set off for Bethlehem.

Mary Mary and Joseph had understood the dream well. When Mary was well enough to walk, they began their escape out of Bethlehem.

Joseph The night was black, with not a star in the sky.

  Darkness. A mass entry of Soldiers with swords.

They were still leaving the town when the soldiers arrived.

  The Soldiers arrive, crossing down the main streets.

Soldiers rushed past on all sides!
  The crunch of boots, the rattle of metal on metal, filled their ears!

Mary Mary clung to her new-born child with all the love in her heart.

  The baby cries.

Don't cry, little one.

Joseph The soldiers blocked all the gates of the town. There was no way out.

The Soldiers start to search the town.

We must hide.

The baby cries again.

Mary Don't cry, little one!

Joseph Where can we hide?

They find somewhere.
Doors are opened and sabres thrust into corners.

Joseph The soldiers began knocking on doors.

Mary They tore through the town!

Joseph Doors were smashed down.

Mary Families were ripped apart!

Joseph Every new-born baby was taken from its parents and slain.

Mary The crying of mothers and fathers and the screaming of the terrified babies echoed through the streets.

Joseph The town was filled with the sound of pure horror.

A cacophony of noise and screaming grows and grows as the culling takes place. This is the Massacre of the Innocents.
The baby cries.

Soldiers What was that?

The baby cries. The soldiers freeze. A deadly tension.

Soldier Did you hear that? A baby's cry.

Soldier Where's it coming from?

The baby cries again.

Soldier Here!

Soldier I think there's one here! There is!

Mary But when the soldier laid eyes on the child he froze and his voice changed.

Soldier No, I was mistaken. There is no one here.

The other Soldiers disperse. He falls to the ground.

Forgive me, my Lord.

The Soldier leaps up and shows them the way.

Soldier This way.

Joseph Run!

Mary They ran as fast as Mary could manage.

Joseph Through narrow streets, across marketplaces, through arches, down alleys, through gates and gardens, until . . .

Mary (*exhausted*) Finally . . .

Joseph They reached freedom!

Mary They climbed a small hill and looked back down on the town as the killing continued faster and bloodier than ever.

*Another bout of killing, more horrific than ever.
A strange music intervenes.*

Joseph But then something miraculous happened.

The souls of the dead children appear.

Mary As each innocent life was taken, the soul of the dead baby soared above its body and flew into the heavens to become a bright and burning star.

The stars rise.

Joseph A night sky of stars the like of which had never been seen glistened above Bethlehem.

Mary And the soldiers gazed in wonder at the heavens and said to each other:

Soldiers This is a miracle.

Herod Herod watched in terror from his balcony in Jerusalem as thousands of stars rose from Bethlehem to settle in the gleaming firmament above him. They looked down on him as the innocent look down on the guilty.
And Herod knew then that he was defeated, and damned to eternal shame

He flees through the palace corridors, screaming.
The sky of stars makes music of heavenly love as Herod flees in the madness of evil.

Mary High above Bethlehem the souls of the children glistened like small tears.

Joseph Or like jewels!

Mary Mary looked at Joseph with a deep love. Her muscles ached, her bones stung with pain, but her heart sang!

Joseph And as they stared into each other's eyes . . .

Mary The angel appeared once more . . .

They see the Angel.

The Angel Because you had faith, because you kept hope in your hearts, because you loved each other, he was born. Because he was born, the innocents killed tonight shall take their place in the heavens. And all future generations shall gaze at the stars and know that, though the guilty may always massacre the innocent, the innocent shall always be victorious.

Mary A breeze rose through the desert trees.

Joseph As it had to Joseph that first night when he had first doubted Mary's word.

Mary . . .
And a word hung on the breeze.

All Believe!

The End.

GREAT EXPECTATIONS

adapted from the novel by Charles Dickens

Great Expectations was first performed on 11 April 2003 at Bristol Old Vic. The cast was as follows:

Pip Aidan McArdle
Magwitch Simon Wolfe
Joe Sam Cox
Mrs Joe/Biddy Sophie Duvall
Miss Haversham/Mrs Hubble Jenny Quayle
Jaggers/Pumblechook Adrian Schiller
Drummle/Compeyson Simon Chadwick
Estella/Hubble Rachel Ferjani

Director Gordon Anderson
Designer Dick Bird
Lighting Neil Austin
Sound Nick Manning
Movement Dan O'Neill
Assistant Director Emma Stuart
Dialect Coach Neil Swain
Casting Director Sam Chandley

Characters

Pip
Magwitch
Joe
Mrs Joe
Biddy
Pumblechook
Hubble
Mrs Hubble
Miss Haversham
Estella
Jaggers
Wemmick
Drummle
Compeyson
Wopsle
Mr Trabb
Miss Havisham's Relations
Members of the Finches
Old Woman
Young Man
A Jew
Boatman
Sergeant
Soldiers
Tailors

Prologue

December 1845. Dusk. A graveyard on the North Kent
marshes. A bleak place, thick with mist, overgrown with
nettles, peppered by tombstones and crucifixes, including
one stone more prominent than the others . . .
Enter a puppet – a boy of seven years old – through
the mist. The puppet-boy is dressed in simple country
rags. He goes to the grave and prays.

Man's Voice (*from off*) Pip? Where are you, Pip?

Enter a man in his mid- to late thirties. Well dressed
in smart gentleman's clothes. He is (also) Pip. Our
Pip. On entering the churchyard he stops, seeing the
puppet sitting before the particular tombstone. The
puppet-boy beckons Pip over to the gravestone. Pip
reads the gravestone.

Pip 'Here lies Philip Pirrip, late of this parish, and also
Georgiana, wife of the above.'

Pause.

Let me set you up upon the stone.

Pip helps the puppet-boy clamber up on the tombstone.
Pip turns away to stare at the sea.
The boy, perched upon it, takes out a crust of bread
and starts to eat it ravenously. When Pip turns back to
see this, he stops, as if struck by a tremendous shock
of memory.
Suddenly a dark shadow can be seen towering up
from behind the tombstone, over the unsuspecting
puppet-boy. The figure towers taller and taller, and

*then seems to plunge down to grab the puppet-boy by
the neck and literally to tear him apart . . . Pip screams
and runs to fight the man, but as he does so, the
puppet-boy seems to disappear in pieces and Pip, his
rich clothes ripped from him to reveal identical rags to
the boy-puppet, takes his place in the arms of Abel
Magwitch . . .*

Act One

The same graveyard. December 1819. Dusk. Magwitch is suddenly grabbing Pip, who is dressed exactly as the puppet-boy in the Prologue, and is now (playing) seven years old. He is screaming.

Magwitch Keep still, you little devil, or I'll cut your throat!

Pip Don't cut my throat, sir! Pray don't do it, sir!

Magwitch Tell us your name. Quick!

Pip Pip, sir.

Magwitch Give it mouth!

Pip Pip! Pip, sir!

Magwitch Show us where you live.

Pip In the v-village, sir.

> *Pip points. Magwitch turns him upside down to see what is in his pockets, which is a crust of bread. Magwitch eats ravenously, perched on the tombstone.*

Magwitch You young dog, what fat cheeks you got! I have half a mind to eat them! Where's your mother?

Pip (*pointing*) There, sir.

> *Pause as Magwitch looks and runs round in shock.*

Magwitch Where?!

Pip There sir. 'Also Georgiana.'

Magwitch That's your mother?

Pip Yes, sir.

Magwitch And is that your father along with your mother?

Pip Yes, sir. 'Philip Pirrip. Late of this parish.'

Magwitch And you were attending to their grave, were you, boy?

Pip Yes, sir.

Magwitch That being something you do often . . .

Pip Yes, sir.

Magwitch Being as you miss 'em so.

Pip I never saw 'em, sir. Not my mother or my father, sir.

Magwitch Who'd you live with, supposin' you're kindly let to live, which I han't made up my mind about?

Pip My sister, sir – Mrs Joe Gargery – wife of Joe Gargery the blacksmith, sir!

Magwitch Blacksmith, eh? Now lookee 'ere, the question being whether you're to be let to live. You know what a file is?

Pip Yes, sir.

Magwitch And you know what wittles are?

Pip Yes, sir. Food, sir.

Magwitch You get me a file. And you get me wittles. You bring 'em to me. Are you hearing me, boy?

Pip If you would kindly please to let me keep upright, sir, perhaps I shouldn't be sick, and perhaps I could attend more.

Magwitch You bring them here tomorrow morning. You do it and you never say a word or dare to make a sign concerning your having seen such a person as me or any person similar, and you shall be let to live. You fail, and your heart and liver shall be tore out, roast and ate. Now, what do you say?

Pip I'll get you the file.

Magwitch And the wittles!

Pip And the wittles.

Magwitch Lord strike you dead!

Pip Lord strike me dead!

Magwitch Now go!

Pip Good – goodnight, sir!

Magwitch Much of that! I wish I were a frog! Or a eel!

TWO

Pip sprints home in terror as Magwitch remains as a shadow behind. We are in the kitchen at Mrs Joe Gargery's. A glowing fire. Joe seated, cleaning up from work. Pip entering slyly.

Joe Mrs Joe has been out a dozen times looking for you, Pip. And she's out now making it a baker's dozen.

Pip Is she?

Joe And I'm sorry to say she's got Tickler with her. She sot down and she got up and she made a grab at Tickler and she ram-paged out. She ram-paged out, Pip.

Pip Has she been gone long, Joe?

Joe Well, she's been on the ram-page, this last spell, about five minutes, Pip. (*Pause.*) She's coming! Get behind the door, old chap!

Enter Mrs Joe on the ram-page, with apron and tickler (a piece of wax-ended cane) as Pip hides behind the door.

Mrs Joe Where is he?

As the door won't fully open, Mrs Joe discovers Pip's whereabouts and beats him with the tickler, then throws him towards Joe, who fences him behind his leg.

Where have you been, you young monkey? Tell me directly what you've been doing to wear me away with fret and fright and worry, or I'll have you out of that corner if you was fifty Pips and he was five hundred Gargerys.

Pip I have only been to the churchyard.

Mrs Joe Churchyard! If it wasn't for me, you'd have been to the churchyard long ago! Who brought you up by hand?

Pip You did.

Mrs Joe And why did I do it, I'd like to know?

Pip I don't know.

Mrs Joe *I* don't! I know this: I'd never do it again! Now sit there and eat your tea. Churchyard indeed! (*Mrs Joe butters some crusty bread and hands it out. Laying out the buttered bread*) Churchyard! You'll drive me to the churchyard, one of these days.

Pip does not touch his food.

Joe Are you not hungry, Pip?

Pip Yes.

Mrs Joe Then eat, boy. Eat!

Joe chews silently as Mrs Joe makes herself busy. Pip suddenly hides the bread down his trousers. Joe looks up to see that it is suddenly gone.

Joe I say, you know, Pip, old chap. You'll do yourself a mischief.

Mrs Joe What's the matter?

Joe It'll stick somewhere, Pip. You can't have chawed it.

Mrs Joe What's the matter now?

Joe If you can cough up any of it, I'd recommend it. Manners is manners, but elth is elth.

Mrs Joe (*grabbing Joe by the neck*) I said what's the matter, you staring great stuck pig?

Joe (*in her vice-like grasp*) You know, Pip. You and me is always friends and I'd be the last to tell on you at any time. But such a, such a most uncommon bolt as that!

Pause.

Mrs Joe Been bolting his food, has he?

Joe I mean, I bolted myself when I was a boy.

Mrs Joe Right, you, you come and be dosed.

Mrs Joe grabs Pip. Mrs Joe takes a huge bottle from the pantry and opens it. Mrs Joe pours it down his throat. And pours. And pours. Gulls scream overhead. Pip screams silently as the tar is forced down his throat. Gulls scream. Pip's silent scream.
A sudden rumble of guns.

Joe That's another convict off.

243

Pip (*still in Mrs Joe's grasp*) What does that mean, Joe?

Mrs Joe (*strangling him*) Escaped. Escaped!

Pip (*mouthing silently to Joe*) What's a convict?

Joe There was a convict off last night. And now, it appears, there's another.

Pip Who's firing?

Mrs Joe Drat that boy! What a questioner he is!

Pause.

Pip Mrs Joe. I should like to know where the firing comes from.

Mrs Joe From the hulks!

Pip Oh, the hulks. (*Pause.*) What's hulks?

Mrs Joe That's the way with this boy! Answer him one question and he'll ask you a dozen directly! Hulks are prison ships.

Pip I wonder who are put in prison ships . . .

Mrs Joe Why, people who begin by asking questions and end up committing murder and robbery!

Pip leaves the scene and is suddenly alone.

Pip Robbery! Robbery! Robbery!

THREE

Pip is running through the mists carrying the bread he stole, a bottle and a pork pie.
Now at the graveyard sits the shadow. His back to us. Pip approaches him.

Pip Sir?

The shadow turns. It is not Magwitch, but another convict. Younger, with a scar on his cheek. The man pushes Pip over. Pip covers himself and screams, awaiting imminent disembowelment. The man runs. Pause. Magwitch appears. Pip rises in terror.

Magwitch What's in the bottle, boy?

Pip . . .

Magwitch I said what's in that bottle?

Pip B-b-brandy, sir. I took it from our pantry. And here's bread and a p-p-pie. A p-pork p-pie. I took that too.

Magwitch eats and drinks, shivering. Pause.

I'm glad you enjoy it.

Magwitch Did you speak?

Pip I said I'm glad you enjoyed it.

Magwitch Thankee, boy, I do. (*Beat.*) It be Christmas tomorrow, be it not, boy? Well then, you've given me my Christmas dinner.

Pip I am afraid you won't leave any of it for him.

Magwitch Him? Who's him?

Pip Your friend?

Magwitch Friend? What friend?

Pip He was just here. He was dressed like you . . . and with the same reason for borrowing a file.

Magwitch Then there *was* firing . . . Did you notice anything in him?

Pip He had a badly bruised face.

Magwitch Not here?

Pip Yes. there.

Magwitch Where is he? Show me the way he went. I'll pull him down a like a bloodhound! Curse this iron! Give us the file boy! Give it to us! (*And Magwitch starts sawing with the file like a madman.*)

FOUR

The forge. Mrs Joe is sawing at a joint of pork like a madwoman. Now appearing like ghosts popping up from a graveyard are the guests – a macabre selection of village life, like a line of pallid ghouls at a feast of the dead . . .

It is Christmas meal. Around the table are Pumblechook, Wopsle, Hubble, Mrs Hubble, Joe and, perched on a corner, low down, Pip. They are intoning a prayer. A large roast pig on the table.

Wopsle For what we are about to receive, may the Lord make us truly grateful.

All Amen.

Mrs Joe Do you hear that boy? Be grateful.

Pumblechook Especially be grateful, boy, to them which brought you up by hand.

Mrs Hubble Why is it that the young are never grateful?

Hubble Naturally wicious.

All (*except Pip and Joe*) True. True.

Pumblechook Why do you insist on staring at the pantry door, boy?

Pip N-no reason, sir.

Pumblechook You're not keeping secrets, I hope?

Pip N-no, sir. Really, sir.

Pumblechook Because you know what happens to boys who keep secrets. Dark secrets. Festering in the mind. In the dank recesses of the soul.

Hubble What, may I ask, are the assembled company's thoughts on the parson's Christmas sermon?

Wopsle Rot, Mr Hubble! An ill-chosen and inexcusable homily!

All (*except Joe and Pip*) True, Mr Wopsle. True.

Wopsle You would not have heard me delivering such a sermon on such an occasion. And less excusable given the surfeit of suitable subjects going about.

Pumblechook True again. You've hit it, sir! A man needn't go far to find a subject these days.

Mrs Joe Indeed not, Mr Pumblechook.

Pumblechook Look at pork alone. There's a subject! If you want a subject, look at pork!

Wopsle Many a moral for the young might be deduced from that text.

Mrs Joe (*to Pip*) You listen to this.

Wopsle Swine were the companions of the prodigal. What is detestable in a pig is more detestable in a boy!

Hubble Or girl.

Wopsle Of course, or girl, Mr Hubble. But there is no girl present.

Pumblechook Besides, think what you've got to be grateful for. If you'd been born a squeaker.

Mrs Joe He was if ever boy was.

Pumblechook But I mean a four-footed squeaker. If you had been born pig, boy, would you have been here now? Not you . . .

Wopsle Unless in that form . . .

Pumblechook (*angry*) But I don't mean in that form. I mean, enjoying himself with his elders and betters, and improving himself with their conversation and rolling in the lap of luxury. Would he have been doing that? No, he wouldn't. And what would have been your destination? You would have been disposed of for so many shillings according to the market price of the article and Dunstable the butcher would have come up to you as you lay in your straw and he would have whipped you under his left arm and with his right would have taken a penknife from under his pocket and he would have put it to your neck and shed your blood and had your life! No bringing up by hand then. Not a bit of it!

The table suddenly transforms (in Pip's mind) into a posse of grunting, snarling, blade-wielding butchers, with Pip as the pig. Then the image disappears, and as civilised as you like . . .

Mrs Joe Have a little brandy, Uncle.

Pip Brandy!

Pumblechook Why yes, a little brandy would not be unwelcome.

Pip holds tight to the leg of the table under the cloth and awaits his fate. In what seems to take an eternity, Mrs Joe fetches the brandy. Uncle Pumblechook pours

a glass, then swills it in his glass, smells it slowly like
a connoisseur, smiles knowingly and, at last, at last! –
drinks. Then he springs to his feet, whoops
spasmodically, turns, twists several times and rushes
out the door, where he can be seen violently plunging
and expectorating. Then he returns and emits one
significant gasp.

Tar!

Mrs Joe Tar?

Pumblechook Tar!

Mrs Joe Why, how ever . . .?

Pause.

Pumblechook It's nothing! No, really . . .

Mrs Joe But, Uncle . . .

Pumblechook I won't hear a word!

Wopsle But tar!

Mrs Joe Wait . . .

Hubble/Mrs Hubble Are you . . .?

Pumblechook No really.

Hubble/Mrs Hubble Poor man . . .

Pumblechook Not at all.

All But tar!

Pumblechook I should be going . . .

Wopsle I should be going . . .

Hubble/Mrs Hubble We should be going . . .

Mrs Joe No! Wait!! Clean plates, Joe!

Pip grabs the table again.

You must taste . . .

Pip Must they?

Mrs Joe You must all at least taste . . .

Pip Must they? Must they really taste it?

Mrs Joe . . . such a delightful and delicious present of Uncle Pumblechook's. It's a savoury pie. A . . .

Pip/Mrs Joe Pork pie!

Pause.

Pumblechook (*clearing his mouth*) Well, Mrs Joe, we'll do our best endeavours. Let us have a cut at this same pie.

Mrs Joe goes to fetch the pie. Her steps echo through the house like the walk of the dead. This all from Pip's perspective, everything distorted, larger than life . . . Mr Pumblechook balances his knife. Mr Wopsle pats his stomach. Mr Hubble licks his lips. Mrs Hubble moistens.

Joe (*bizarrely loud and stretched out*) You shall have some, Pip.

They all sharpen their knives as if it is Pip they are to set upon. Pip runs for his life, opens the front door and bumps straight into a soldier.

Pip Aaaaah!

Soldiers Where's the criminal? The criminal! The criminal!

Suddenly there seem to be soldiers everywhere, in waterproofs covering their heads. They wheel the

*screaming Pip up in the air and for a second seem as
if they are going to lynch him from a convenient post
as a common criminal . . . a robber!*

    *But suddenly Pip is on Joe's shoulders, and we are
out in the marshes . . .*

FIVE

*On the marshes by the churchyard. Darkness. Soldiers
with torches. Amidst them Pip and Joe. Sleet and rain
pouring down.*

Soldiers No one here, sir. / Not here, sir.

Sergeant They're pretty well known to be out here still.
They'll find themselves trapped in a circle sooner than
they can count on.

    Shouts from a distance. The Soldiers stop dead.

Eastwards. By the shore! Run!

    They run on into the marshes. As they run . . .

Voice Murder!

Magwitch Convicts! Runaways! This way for the
runaway convicts!

    *Suddenly the two convicts appear fighting, sprawled
on the ground.*

Sergeant Here they are! Surrender, you two!

    A great fight. The Soldiers rush in and separate them.

Magwitch Mind! I took him! I give him up to you!
Mind that!

Sergeant It'll do you small good, my man. Handcuffs!

Magwitch I don't expect it to do me any good! I took him. He knows it! That's enough for me!

Compeyson Take notice, guard. He tried to murder me.

Magwitch Tried to murder him? Try, and not do it! Given him up, that's what I done! Dragged him 'ere! Single-handed I got clear of the prison ship. I could ha' got clear of these death-cold flats. But let *him* go free? Let him profit by means as I found out? Let him make a tool of me afresh and again? No no no!

Sergeant Enough.

Magwitch If I'd had died, I'd have held to him with that grip that you should have been safe to find him in my hold!

The Sergeant fires in the air.

Sergeant Enough!

Magwitch sees Pip. Pause. Pip very slowly shakes his head and makes a small gesture with his hands. Magwitch stares at him.

Take them away.

Magwitch Wait. I wish to say something respecting this escape. A man can't starve; at least I can't. I took up some wittles, up at the village over yonder – where the church stands almost out on the marshes.

Sergeant You mean stole.

Magwitch And I'll tell you where from. From the blacksmith's. A dram of liquor and a pie.

Sergeant Have you happened to miss such an article as a pie, blacksmith?

Joe My wife did, at the very moment you came in. Don't you know, Pip?

Magwitch So you're the blacksmith. Then I'm sorry to say I ate your pie.

Magwitch stares at Pip.

Sergeant Take them to the landing boat.

The Soldiers take Magwitch and the other convict and march them away. But as they do, Magwitch turns back and stares at Pip once more. He holds out his huge hands as he stares at him and makes the same gesture Pip made to him. Pip recoils. They stare at each other with a gaze that lasts long and lingers deep into the darkness . . .

SIX

A year later. Pip and Joe are alone at the forge. Pip is writing on a slate as Joe dozes.

Pip Joe. Wake up, Joe.

Joe Hmmmn! What is it?

Pip I've written you an epistle.

Joe A whattle, Pip?

Pip A letter, Joe. From me to you.

Pip hands Joe a slate on which is written 'Mi DEER JO i Ope U r KWITE wELL'.

Joe I say, Pip old chap! What a scholar you are!

Pip I should like to be.

Joe Why here's a J! And an O equal to anythink! Here's a J and an O, Pip, and a J-O. JOE! Astonishing. You *are* a scholar.

Pip How do you spell Gargery, Joe?

Joe I don't spell it at all.

Pip But supposing you did.

Joe It can't be supposed. Tho' I am oncommon fond of reading.

Pip Are you?

Joe Oncommon. Give me a good book or a good newspaper and sit me down afore a good fire and I ask no better.

Pip Didn't you ever go to school when you were as little as me?

Joe Well, Pip, I'll tell you. My father, he were given to drink, and when he were overtook with it, he hammered my mother. It were almost the only hammering he did, 'cepting at myself. Consequence, my mother ran away with me several times and she'd go out to work and she'd say, 'Joe, now please God, you shall have some schooling,' and put me in a school. But my father were that good in his heart that he couldn't abear to be without us. He'd come with a tremendous crowd, grab us by our necks, and then he'd take us home, and hammer us again. Which you see, Pip, were a drawback on my learning.

Pip But why . . .

Joe Why don't I learn now?

Pip Yes, Joe.

Joe Well, your sister ain't over-partial to having scholars on the premises.

Suddenly the bells of a carriage ring out. Enter Mrs Joe and Pumblechook.

254

Mrs Joe Now if this boy ain't grateful this night, he never will be. It's only to be hoped he won't be pompeyed.

Pumblechook She ain't in that line, mum. She knows better.

Pip (*mouth to Joe*) She?

Joe (*mouth to Pip*) She?

Mrs Joe Well, what are you staring at? Is the house afire?

Joe Which some individual . . . mentioned 'she'?

Mrs Joe Well, she is a 'she', I suppose. Unless you call Miss Havisham a 'he'.

Joe Miss Havisham up town?

Mrs Joe Is there a Miss Havisham down town?

Pumblechook She wants the boy to go and play there.

Mrs Joe And he'd better play there. Or I'll work him.

Pumblechook Have you heard of Miss Havisham, boy?

Pip I think I have, sir.

Pumblechook What have you heard?

Pip That she is very rich and very grim and that her house is very large and very dismal.

Pumblechook Miss Havisham lives in magnificent seclusion. Her windows are boarded and barred. Her rooms are dark and secret. No one is asked to attend her. No one! But you are asked, boy. You are asked to play.

Pause as they all stare at him.

Pip What will I play?

SEVEN

*A room in Miss Havisham's house. It is almost totally
dark. Pip stands in terror. Suddenly he sees in an armchair
Miss Havisham, dressed in white, rich materials, satins,
lace and silks. White shoes, only one on. White veil from
her hair.*

Miss Havisham Who is it?

Pip Pip, ma'am. Come to play.

Miss Havisham Come nearer. Let me look at you. (*Pip
approaches gingerly.*) You are not afraid of a woman
who has never seen the sun since you were born?

Pip No, ma'am.

Miss Havisham Do you know what I touch here?

Pip Yes, ma'am.

Miss Havisham What do I touch?

Pip Your heart.

Miss Havisham Broken!

  Pause.

This was my dressing room. What do you think of it?

Pip I . . . I . . .

Miss Havisham It has not seen a glimpse of daylight
since that day. Since that hour. Twenty to nine. (*showing
her watch*) Twenty to nine!

  *Pip looks round to see other clocks swooping from
  the darkness and also stopped at twenty to nine.*

I am tired. I want diversion and I have done with men
and women. Play.

Pip (*looking round at the dim expanse of room*) Play, ma'am?

Miss Havisham I sometimes have sick fancies. And I have a sick fancy that I want to see some play. There. There! Play! Play! Play!

Pause.

Are you sullen and obstinate?

Pip No, ma'am. I am very sorry for you and very sorry I can't play just now. It's so new here, and so strange, and so fine, and so melancholy.

Miss Havisham So new to him. So old to me. So strange to him, so familiar to me. So melancholy to both of us. (*Pause.*) Go to the door. Call Estella.

Pip Who?

Miss Havisham Estella! You can do that, can't you?

Pip (*at the door, into the darkness*) Estella!

Miss Havisham Louder.

Pip Estella!

Miss Havisham She won't hear if you whimper! Louder! Louder!!

Pip Estella! Estella!!

Enter Estella out of the darkness. A very pretty girl of Pip's age, beautifully dressed. She approaches Miss Havisham, who shows her a jewel from her dressing table.

Miss Havisham Your own, one day, my dear, and you will use it well. Let me see you play cards with this boy.

Estella But he's just a common labouring boy!

Miss Havisham (*quietly*) Well? You can break his heart.

Estella What do you play, boy?

Pip Nothing but beggar-my-neighbour, miss.

Miss Havisham Beggar him!

They play, she winning. Time passes with only Estella occasionally saying 'Beggared' punctuating the stretching of time . . . Pip is far more interested in her than the game, and only stops when she catches him staring . . .

Pip Is that your knave, miss, or mine?

Estella (*loud*) He calls the jacks knaves, this boy! And what coarse hands he has! And what thick boots!

Pip stares at his hands. Estella beggars him.

There! I've beggared him again!

Miss Havisham How does he play?

Estella As clumsily as could be imagined. Your deal, boy.

But as Pip picks up the cards, he makes an utter mess of the deal.

You stupid, clumsy, labouring boy!

Estella takes the cards away from him, throws some at him, and stands, dancing slowly round the room and throwing the rest of the cards into the air.

Miss Havisham (*to Pip*) You say nothing of her. She says many hard things of you, but you say nothing of her. What do you think of her?

Pip I don't like to say.

Miss Havisham Tell me in my ear.

Pip I think she is very proud.

Miss Havisham Anything else?

Pip I think she is very pretty.

Miss Havisham Anything else?

Pip I think she is very insulting.

Miss Havisham Anything else?

Pip I think I should like to go home now.

Miss Havisham And never see her again, even though she is so pretty?

Pip I am not sure that I shouldn't like to see her again but I should like to go home now.

Miss Havisham When shall I have you again?

Pip Today is Wednesday . . .

Miss Havisham There there! I know nothing of days of the week! Come again after six days, you hear? Estella, take him down. Let him have something to eat, and let him go.

> *Exit Havisham. Estella leads Pip out, whistling at him like a dog. The courtyard is full of empty casks of bee that stand like gravestones.*

Estella This is the brewery.

Pip Yes, miss.

Estella Better not try to brew beer here now, or it would turn sour, boy, don't you think?

Pip It looks like it, miss.

Estella Not that anybody means to try. For Satis House will stand idle as it is, until it falls.

DAVID FARR

Pip Is that the name of the house?

Estella It is Greek, or Latin, or Hebrew, or all three, for 'enough'.

Pip Enough House.

Estella (*close to him now*) Enough!

Estella starts to dance gracefully around on the old casks of beer, from cask to cask . . .

Estella Won't you dance, boy?

Pip I don't dance, miss.

Estella Common labouring boy.

She flits in and out from between the casks like a half-glimpsed apparition. It is an image of grace and beauty. Pip turns away from her, crying.
Now Estella is beside him, placing a bowl of food on the ground as you would for a dog.

Eat up, there's a good boy! (*She laughs.*) Why don't you cry, boy?

Pip I don't want to.

Estella Yes, you do. You have been crying and when I'm gone you'll cry until you are half-blind!

And she leaves him. Pip stands alone, trying not to cry. Then, and with great suddenness, he rushes like a dog to bury his head in the bowl like a dog, snuffling, bow-wow-wowing like a crazed hound, and crying his eyes out . . .

EIGHT

The classroom at Great Aunt Wopsle's House. Desks.
Biddy, a twelve-year-old girl, is sweeping up. Pip enters
with his school bag.

Biddy I thought you had gone home, Pip. School is
finished for today.

Pip Biddy, I need to speak to you.

Biddy I am listening.

Pip Biddy, I need you to make me uncommon.

Biddy How do I do that, Pip? I am only a common
orphan girl myself.

Pip You taught me the alphabet as much as I could learn
it. Well, now I need to know more so that I may be teach'd
like a gentleman.

Biddy But you are taught here in the school.

Pip Here? All that happens here is your grandmother
Wopsle beats us with a birch and hands out the book,
which has no pages left in it anyway, and then she falls
into a coma and we all eat apples and put straws up
each others' backs, and discover who can tread hardest
on whose boots, until you make a rush at us with the
three Bibles and we all read aloud without having any
idea what we are saying and then Great Aunt Wopsle
wakes up and pulls someone's ears and we all go home.
I need a real teacher and since the little I have learnt
I have learnt from you, I should like you, Biddy, to be
my teacher. You could teach me in evenings so as I become
taught and uncommon, see?

Biddy I am only twelve, Pip. I have much learning to do
of my own.

Pip One evening a week, Biddy, and I shall get on in life, I know I will.

Biddy Is it of great importance to you, Pip?

Pip It is of the greatest importance, Biddy, and for a partic'lar reason that I shall not tell.

Biddy Then I shall teach you.

Pip Oh Biddy, thank you. Thank you.

NINE

Miss Havisham's: the decaying dining room. A long table covered in white cloth, with seemingly moving mould and decay all over. Miss Havisham is with a smartly dressed gentleman. The gentleman, we shall later learn, is Mr Jaggers.

Miss Havisham It is possible?

Jaggers Most possible.

Miss Havisham I want them to get nothing. Nothing!

Jaggers Then nothing they shall get.

Pip enters.

Miss Havisham Ah, Pip, there you are. Come in, the gentleman and I have completed our business.

Jaggers Good day, Miss Havisham.

Miss Havisham Good day.

At which, the man turns and, giving Pip a piercing stare and a short bow, leaves, so that Pip and Miss Havisham are alone.

Pip Who was . . . ?

Miss Havisham So, the days have worn away, have they?

Pip Yes ma'am. Today is . . .

Miss Havisham There! There! I don't want to know.

Pip What is this room, ma'am?

Miss Havisham The dining room. Spacious, isn't it? It was handsome once. What ails you, boy?

Pip The air, ma'am. I find it hard to breathe.

Miss Havisham Are you ready to play?

Pip I don't think I am, ma'am.

Miss Havisham Not at cards again?

Pip I suppose. If I was wanted.

Miss Havisham Since you are unwilling to play, are you willing to work?

Pip Oh yes, ma'am, I am quite willing.

Miss Havisham Walk me.

They start to walk at quite a lick around the room, circling the long table. This continues for a while . . . then she stops and bangs the table with her stick.

This is where I will be laid when I am dead. They shall come and look at me here. (*Points with her stick to a great centrepiece, whose form is quite indistinguishable.*) What do you think that is, there where those cobwebs are?

Pip I can't guess what it is, ma'am.

Miss Havisham It's a great cake. A bride-cake. Mine! On this day of the year, long before you were born, this heap of decay was brought here. It and I have worn away together. The mice have gnawed it and sharper teeth than mice have gnawed at me!

A noise. Spiders rush out from under the cake. Miss Havisham freezes.

Here they come, Pip. Walk me. Walk me!

A group of grotesque relations gather at the door muttering 'Many happy returns,' bowing and smiling obsequiously.

Relations Miss Havisham, dear Miss Havisham, congratulations Miss Havisham, sweet Miss Havisham.

Relation 1 Dear Miss Havisham. How well you look!

Miss Havisham I do not. I am yellow skin and bone.

Relation 2 Poor dear soul. Certainly not to be considered to look well, poor thing. The idea!

Relations The idea! The idea! The very idea!

Miss Havisham And how are you?

Relation 3 Thank you, Miss Havisham. I am as well as is to be expected.

Miss Havisham Why, what's the matter with you?

Relation 3 Nothing worth mentioning. I don't wish to make a display of my feelings, but I have habitually thought of you more in the night than I am equal to.

Miss Havisham Then don't think of me.

Relations Very easily said! Very easily said!

Relation 4 (*to Relation 3*) My dear, it is well known that your family feelings are gradually undermining you to the extent of making one leg shorter than the other.

Relation 3 Without expecting any thanks of any sort . . .

Relations   No, no thanks. No thanks. No thanks.

Miss Havisham stops walking.

Miss Havisham   You shall receive thanks! – all of you! When I am laid on that table! That will be your place! At my head. And yours will be there! And your husband's there! And you there! Now you all know where to take your stations when you come to feast on me! And now go! (*to Pip*) Walk me! Walk me!

Relations   Goodbye, Miss Havisham. / Farewell, Miss Havisham. / Dear Miss Havisham. / Sweet Miss Havisham . . .

The relations fade as they came. Miss Havisham continues to walk and then stops.

Miss Havisham   This is my birthday, Pip. I don't suffer those that were here just now or anyone to speak of it. When the ruin is complete and when they lay me dead, in my bride's dress on the bride's table, which shall be done and which will be the finished curse upon him – so much the better if it is done on this day! (*Pause.*) Call Estella.

Pip   (*screaming into the darkness*) Estella! Estella!!

Estella enters. Pause.

Miss Havisham   (*to Pip*) Does she grow prettier and prettier, Pip?

Pip   Yes, ma'am, I believe she does.

Miss Havisham   (*to Estella*) Break their hearts, my pride and hope, break their hearts and have no mercy! Ha ha ha. I feel merry. There. There. Sing!

Pip   Sing, ma'am?

Miss Havisham   Sing a song.

Pip I know no songs, ma'am.

The shadow of Joe appears humming a tune.

That is to say I only know of one song.

Miss Havisham Then sing it!

Pip It's a common forge song, ma'am. It's not right for a house such as this.

Miss Havisham I said sing it. Sing it!

Joe is singing as he strikes iron at the forge.

Joe (*singing*)
Hammer boysaround. Old Clem!
With a thump and a sound. Old Clem!
Beat it out, beat it out. Old Clem!
With a clink for the stout. Old Clem!
Blow the fire, blow the fire. Old Clem!
Roaring dryer, soaring higher. Old Clem!

Pip joins in the song, singing it to Miss Havisham. He starts to walk her, and she to sing it too with great enthusiasm. Now Estella joins in, and the three dance round the room to the blacksmith's ditty, faster and faster to the increasing tempo of Joe's anvil-beat. Then Miss Havisham speaks over . . .

Miss Havisham Now listen to me, Pip. You shall return every alternate day at noon, for as long as I deem necessary. You may be assured this will be a matter of months at least. Estella will always be about to let you in and out. And you will play. Sometimes she will coldly tolerate you. Sometimes she will condescend to you. Sometimes she will be quite familiar. On one occasion she will tell you energetically –

Estella I hate you! I hate you, common labouring boy!

Miss Havisham And once . . . just once . . .

Joe continues striking the anvil silently in the background. Estella turns to Pip.

Estella You may kiss me if you like.

He kisses her cheek. Estella stares at Pip in passive amusement as he melts before her.

Miss Havisham Once, like a dog, and never again.

Estella laughs. Miss Havisham, Estella and Joe fade into nothingness and the song ends.

TEN

Eight months later. The Jolly Bargemen pub. Joe and Pumblechook are sitting with a Strange Man, with a pipe and one eye shut as if he were constantly taking aim with an invisible gun.

Strange Man You was saying you was a blacksmith.

Joe Yes, I said it, you know.

Pumblechook He said it because . . .

Strange Man What'll you drink? Mr –? You didn't mention your name.

Joe Gargery.

Strange Man What'll you drink, Mr Gargery?

Joe Well to tell the truth I ain't much in the habit of drinking at anybody's expense except my own.

Strange Man Habit, no. But once and away and on a Saturday night too! Come! Put a name to it, Mr Gargery!

Joe I wouldn't wish to be stiff company. Rum.

Strange Man And will the other gentleman originate a sentiment?

Pumblechook Rum, since offered . . .

Strange Man Three rums!

Pip enters.

Joe Halloa, Pip old chap!

The man offers a place beside him but Pip chooses to sit beside Joe.

Strange Man I am not acquainted with this country, but it seems a solitary country towards the river.

Joe Most meshes is solitary.

Strange Man No doubt. No doubt. Do you find any gypsies, now, or tramps, or vagrants of any sort out there?

Joe None but a runaway convict now and then. And we don't find them easy, do we, Pip?

Strange Man Seems you have been out after such.

Joe Once, two year back. We went out as lookers-on. Didn't we, Pip?

Strange Man He's a likely young parcel of bones, that. What is it you call him?

Joe Pip.

Strange Man Christened Pip?

Joe Not christened Pip.

Strange Man Surname Pip?

Joe No.

Pumblechook Pip is a kind of family name he gave himself when an infant.

Strange Man (*to Joe*) Son of yours?

Joe Well no. No he ain't.

Strange Man Nevvy?

Joe Well – he is not – no, not to deceive you, he is not.

Strange Man Well, what the blue blazes is he?

Pumblechook If I may be so bold, as one who in a position of familial closeness, may pour light on the ties that bind this young boy with Mr Gargery . . .

And Pumblechook continues much in this vein. But we do not hear this, because Pip's attention has been drawn to the Strange Man's stirring of his rum. He is stirring it slowly, and intently, with his eyes fixed only on Pip, and he is stirring it with a file . . .

And that, sir, is as good a way of summing it that you will hear.

Joe And now, if you'll beg us pardon, we'll be making our way home.

Strange Man Stop half a moment, Mr Gargery. I think I've got a bright new shilling somewhere in my pocket and if I have, the boy shall have it.

He finds it, folds it in some crumpled paper and hands it to Pip.

Yours! Mind, your own.

Pip Thank you, sir.

Strange Man Goodnight. Goodnight, sir. Goodnight.

The forge. Joe, Mrs Joe, Pip.

Mrs Joe A bad 'un, I'll be bound. Or he wouldn't have given it to the boy. Let's look at it.

Pip takes out the paper and unfolds it. Pause.

What's this? Two one pound notes!

Pip stares in horror and runs to bed. He tries to sleep. But Pip sees a great hand, with a file, appearing from the door. He strains to see whose hand it is, but soon the image is gone . . .

ELEVEN

Miss Havisham's house. Pip stands alone, hat in hand. Miss Havisham and Estella enter.

Miss Havisham Well, Pip. The months have passed. And now it is time.

Pip Time for what, ma'am?

Miss Havisham Tell me the name of that blacksmith of yours.

Enter Joe dressed up in a smart suit of sorts, terribly nervous.

(*to Joe*) You are the husband of the sister of this boy? (*Pause.*) You are the husband of the sister of this boy?

Joe Which I meantersay, Pip. As I hip and married your sister and I were at that time what you might call if you was always inclined a single man.

Miss Havisham Well! And you have reared the boy with the intention of being your apprentice, is that so, Mr Gargery?

Joe You know, Pip, as you and me were ever friends and it were look'd for'ard to betwixt us, as calc'lated to lead to larks. Not but what, Pip, if you had ever made objections to the business . . .

Miss Havisham Has the boy any objection?

Joe Which it is well beknown to yourself, Pip . . . that it were the wish of your own heart.

Miss Havisham You expected to receive no premium with the boy?

Pip Joe, why don't you answer . . .

Joe Pip. That were not a question to answer betwixt ourselves. You know the answer to be no, and wherefore should I say it?

Miss Havisham Pip has earned a premium here. There are five and twenty guineas in this bag. Give it to your master, Pip.

Joe (*receiving it from Pip*) This is very liberal on your part, Pip, and it is as such received and grateful welcome, though never looked for, far nor near nor nowheres . . . (*Pause.*)

Miss Havisham Goodbye, Pip. Let them out, Estella.

Pip But . . . Am I to come again, Miss Havisham?

Miss Havisham No, Pip.

Pip But Miss Havisham . . .

Miss Havisham Our time is over, Pip.

Pip But Miss Havisham, may I at least visit on occasion?

Miss Havisham No visits!

Pip But I have to!

Joe Now then, Pip.

Pip I have to!

Miss Havisham You shall not! You have served your purpose! (*Pause.*) Gargery is your master now.

Estella and Havisham smile at Pip.

Gargery.

Estella Gargery.

Miss Havisham Gargery!

Pip winces at the sound of the word and squirms into the tightest ball he can muster . . . he tears off his formal visiting clothes . . . blackening himself with coal-dust, darker and darker . . . to the mocking chorus of 'Gargery', 'Gargery' . . .

TWELVE

The forge: Pip is in the forge, in work clothes, blackened, at work, bashing at the anvil. He is bashing away the years. Eleven, twelve, thirteen, fourteen.

Enter Estella in pure white, looking at the coal-black Pip, pointing and laughing. Pip choosing to ignore her, Pip beating the anvil in torture . . . Estella singing the song 'Old Clem' in contempt. Pip beats on and on and on with increasing violence.

As he beats the anvil, his sister crosses the stage, and then, at one of Pip's blows on the anvil, she suddenly falls. Estella disappears into the darkness as the sister is carried to her bed.

Joe She's been taken to her bed, Pip. The doctor says she will not . . . How can I best say it, Pip? She will never ram-page from it again.

Pip Who will look after her, Joe?

Joe We must find someone, Pip. She will need support all day and night. She cannot eat nor drink without help, Pip, and you and I must be working in the forge.

>   *Pause.*

Which I meantersay, Pip, I have asked Miss Biddy to join us to look after Mrs Joe. I hope that is to your liking.

Pip Quite to my liking. (*Pause.*) Are you sad, Joe?

Joe (*hiding his tears*) Which is not to say she couldn't be a Mongol, Pip. She could be. Yes she could.

>   *Joe starts to beat again at the anvil. Pip joins him and they continue their work . . .*

THIRTEEN

>   *On the marshes. Biddy stands alone, waiting. Pip joins her.*

Pip Forgive me, Biddy. I am late.

Biddy I thought perhaps you weren't coming.

Pip Thank you for agreeing to take this walk with me.

Biddy I hope we will have many opportunities to talk now that I am working under the same roof as you.

Pip Yes, we must talk together a little more as we used to.

Biddy I would like that.

>   *Biddy and Pip find a spot to sit and stare out at the sea. Pause.*

Pip Biddy, I want to be a gentleman.

Biddy Oh, I wouldn't if I were you. I don't think it would answer.

Pip Biddy I have very particular reasons for wanting to be a gentleman.

Biddy You know best, Pip, but don't you think you are happier as you are?

Pip Biddy, I am not at all happy as I am. I am disgusted with my calling and my life. I have never taken to either, since I was bound to Joe four years ago. Don't be absurd.

Biddy Was I absurd? I am sorry for that. I only want you to do well and to be comfortable.

Pip Well then, understand once and for all that I shall never or can be comfortable – or anything but miserable – there, Biddy! – unless I can lead a very different life from the life I lead now.

Biddy That's a pity.

Pip If I could have settled down and been but half as fond of the forge as I was when I was little, I know it would have been much better for me. Joe and I would perhaps have gone partners when I was out of my time, and I might even have grown up to keep company with you, and we might have sat on this very bank on a fine Sunday, quite different people. I should have been good enough for *you*: shouldn't I, Biddy?

Biddy Yes, I am not over-particular.

Pip Instead of that, see how I am going on. Dissatisfied and uncomfortable and – what would it signify to me, being coarse and common, if nobody had told me so!

Biddy It was neither a very true nor a very polite thing to say. Who said it?

Pause.

Pip The beautiful young lady at Miss Havisham's all those years ago. And she was more beautiful than anybody ever was, and I admired her dreadfully. And I want to be a gentleman on her account.

Biddy Do you want to be a gentleman to spite her or gain her over?

Pip I don't know.

Biddy Because if it is to spite her I should think – but you know best – that might be better and more independently done by caring nothing for her words. And if it is to gain her over, I should think – but you know best – she was not worth gaining over.

Pip It may be all quite true. But I admire her dreadfully.

Biddy When did you last see her?

Pip Four years ago last month. But I see her every day in my mind.

Pause.

Biddy I am glad of one thing. And that is that you have felt you could give me your confidence, Pip.

Pip Biddy – (*kissing her on the cheek*) I shall always tell you everything.

Biddy Till you're a gentleman.

Pip You know I never shall be, so that's always. Not that I have any occasion to tell you everything, for you know everything I know.

Biddy Ah.

Pip Biddy, I wish you could put me right.

Biddy I wish I could.

Pip If only I could get myself to fall in love with you – you don't mind me speaking so openly with an old acquaintance?

Biddy Oh dear, not at all. Don't mind me.

Pip If I could only get myself to do it, that would be the thing for me!

Biddy But you never will, you see.

They stay in silence as the sea washes up on the shore below them and the birds cry out in the sky. Biddy stares at the sea. Pip looks at her face, then turns to the sea also, where he seems to see Estella circling them, throwing cards with flippant ease and grace.

Pip Pip, what a fool you are.

FOURTEEN

Night. The forge: Joe. Enter Jaggers. The shadows of Miss Havisham and Estella linger in the darkness.

Jaggers I have reason to believe there is a blacksmith amongst you by the name of Gargery, Joseph Gargery. Which is the man?

Joe Here is the man.

Jaggers You have an apprentice commonly known as Pip?

Joe Of four years' serving. I do.

Jaggers Is he here?

Enter Pip and Biddy.

Pip I am here!

Jaggers I wish to have conference with you.

Pip I know you, sir. That is to say we met once.

Jaggers I have no recollection of such a meeting.

Pip We didn't meet. We passed in the dining room of . . . (*He glances at Miss Havisham.*)

Jaggers (*ignoring him*) My name is Jaggers and I am a lawyer in London. I have unusual business to conduct with you and I commence by stating it is business not of my own originating. If my advice had been heeded, I would not have been here. Joseph Gargery, I am the bearer of the offer to relieve you of this young fellow, your apprentice. You would not object to cancel his indentures, at his request and for his own good? You would not want anything for so doing?

Joe Lord forbid that I should want anything for not standing in Pip's way.

Jaggers Lord forbidding is pious but not to the purpose. The question is: do you want anything?

Joe The answer is: no.

Jaggers Very well. Recollect the admission you have made and don't try to go from it presently. Now I return to this young fellow. And the communication I have to make is that he has great expectations. That he will come into a handsome property. Further, that it is the desire of the present possessor of that property that he be immediately removed from his present sphere of life and be brought up a gentleman.

Joe A gentleman?

Pip A gentleman?

> *Pip stares at Miss Havisham. She stares at him inscrutably. He turns to Estella. The same.*

Jaggers Mr Pip. Mr Pip, are you listening to me?

Pip Yes. Yes!

Jaggers I address the rest of what I have to say to you. You are to understand first that it is the request of the person from whom I take my instructions that you always bear the name of Pip. Do you have an objection?

Pip No objection.

Jaggers I should think not. Now you are to understand secondly, Mr Pip, that the name of the person who is your liberal benefactor remains a profound secret until the person chooses to reveal it. Now you are distinctly to understand that you are positively prohibited from making any enquiry on this head, or any allusion or reference, however distant, to any individual, in communications with me. If you have a suspicion in your breast, keep it in your breast. It is not the least to the purpose what the reasons for this prohibition are; they may be the strongest and gravest reasons or they may be mere whim. That is not for you to enquire into. The condition is laid down. Do you have an objection?

Pip No objection.

Jaggers I should think not. Now you are not endowed with expectations only. There is already lodged in my hands a sum of money amply sufficient for your suitable education and maintenance. It is considered that you must be better educated in accordance with your altered position and that you will be alive to the necessity of at once entering on that advantage.

Pip It is what I have always longed for!

Jaggers Never mind what you have always longed for, Mr Pip, keep to the record. If you long for it now, that is enough. When will you come to London?

Pip I suppose I could come directly.

Jaggers First you should have some new clothes to come in, and they should not be working clothes. Say this day week. You'll want some money. Shall I leave you twenty guineas?

He hands them over. Pause.

Well, Joseph Gargery, you look dumbfounded.

Joe I am.

Jaggers It was understood you wanted nothing for yourself, remember?

Joe It were understood and it is understood.

Jaggers But what if it were in my instructions to make you a present, as compensation?

Joe Pip is that hearty welcome to go free with his services, to honour and fortune, as no words can tell him. But if you think as money – can make compensation for me – fur the loss of the little child . . .

Jaggers Now, Joseph Gargery, I warn you, this is your last chance.

Joe Which I meantersay, if you come into my place bull-baiting and badgering me, come out!

Pip Joe.

Joe Which I meantersay as sech if you're a man, come on!

Pip Joe, be quiet.

Joe Which I meantersay that what I say, I meantersay and stand or fall by!

Pip I said be quiet!

DAVID FARR

Pause.

Jaggers Mr Pip, I think the sooner you leave here the better. Let it stand for this day week – and you shall receive my printed address in the meantime.

Jaggers is ready to leave.

Pip Mr Jaggers. I wish to be quite right and keep to your directions. But would there be any objection to my taking leave of anyone before I go.

Jaggers No.

Pip I don't mean in the village, but up town.

Jaggers No objection.

Exit Jaggers. Long pause.

Pip I have always wanted to be a gentleman, and have speculated what I would do if I became one.

Joe Have you, though?

Pip I was thinking, Joe, that when I go down town and order my clothes I shall tell the tailor that I'll come and put them on there. It would be very disagreeable to be stared at by all the people here.

Joe People might like to see you in your new genteel figure . . .

Pip But that's just what I don't want. They would make such a coarse and common business of it that I couldn't bear myself.

Joe Ah, that indeed. If you couldn't bear yourself . . .

Pause.

Pip (*impatient*) Six more days and then the day before the day. They'll soon go.

Joe Yes. They'll soon go.

Pip You may be sure, Joe, that I will never forget you.

Joe No no, Pip. I am sure of that.

Pip It's a pity that you did not get on a little more when we had our lessons here, isn't it?

Joe I don't know. I'm so awful dull. I'm only master of my own trade. It were always a pity as I was so awful dull but it's no more a pity now than it was – this day twelvemonth – don't you see? And now I'll bid you good night, Biddy, and good night, Pip old chap. Good night.

Exit Joe.

Pip Biddy, I have a favour to ask you, and it is that you will not omit any opportunity of helping Joe on a little.

Biddy How helping him on?

Pip For instance in his learning and his manners.

Biddy Won't his manners do, then?

Pip My dear Biddy, they do very well here.

Biddy Oh, they do well here.

Pip Hear me out. But if I were to remove Joe into a higher sphere, as I shall hope to remove him, they would hardly do him justice.

Biddy Don't you think he knows that?

Pip I don't know.

Biddy Have you never considered that he may be proud?

Pip Proud?

Biddy There are many kinds of pride, pride is not all of one kind – (*Pause.*)

Pip Well – why are you stopping?

Biddy He may be too proud to let anyone take him out of a place that he is competent to fill and fills well and with respect. To tell you the truth, I think he is.

Pip I am very sorry to see this in you, Biddy.

Biddy To see what?

Pip You are envious, Biddy, and grudging. You are dissatisfied on account of my rise in fortune, and you can't help showing it.

Biddy If you have the heart to think so, say so. Say so over and over again!

Pip If you have the heart to be so, don't put it off on me! I am sorry for this, Biddy, it's a bad side of human nature. A bad side! As for Joe, after seeing this, I ask you nothing! Nothing!

> *Exit Biddy. Pip looks at his clothes, and in fury tears them from him. Now he enters a reverie. Estella appears and sprays him down with water until he is clean from dirt and coal. Now tailors from all sides appear and towel and dress him in his gentleman's suit and shoes, until he stands like a man reborn.*

FIFTEEN

Miss Havisham's. Miss Havisham and Pip.

Miss Havisham Well, Pip?

Pip I start for London, Miss Havisham, tomorrow and I thought you would not mind me taking leave of you.

Miss Havisham This is a gay figure.

Pip I have come into such good fortune since I saw you last, Miss Havisham. And I am so grateful for it.

Miss Havisham Ay ay. I have seen Jaggers. I have . . . heard about it, Pip. You are adopted by a rich person.

Pip Yes, Miss Havisham.

Miss Havisham Not named.

Pip No, Miss Havisham.

Miss Havisham And Mr Jaggers is made your guardian.

Pip Yes, Miss Havisham.

Miss Havisham Well, you have a promising career before you. Be good. You deserve it.

> *Pause.*

You are looking for Estella?

Pip I merely hoped sh-she was well.

Miss Havisham Abroad. Educating for a lady. Far out of reach. Prettier than ever. Admired by all who see her.

Pip (*smiling*) I believe I will see her soon, Miss Havisham.

Miss Havisham (*also smiling*) You may believe it, Pip. You will always keep the name of Pip, you know.

Pip Yes, Miss Havisham.

Miss Havisham Goodbye, Pip.

> *She stretches out her hand and he goes down on his knee and puts it to his lips.*
>
> *He kisses the hand with a passion, and when he lifts his head, the sound of horses' hooves surrounds him. He is in a carriage hurtling towards London, towards Estella, who is there, waving to him. Pip is radiant,*

*liberated, free, such joy has never been seen on his
young face . . .*

*But as he approaches closer and closer, Estella's
image disappears, and is replaced by a hanged man,
recently executed, strung up on a gibbet outside
Newgate Prison.*

It is an image of sudden ghastly horror.

End of Act One.

Act Two

ONE

London. A sequence in which Pip, in his modest gentleman's suit, is assailed by a multitude of different sellers. He buys lots of new hats, new scarves, new shoes, new jackets, all of increasing extravagance. He is brought in a new chair to sit on, then a plusher one, then an even plusher one. Someone lights him a cigar, someone else gives him a new cane, then a more elegant one still, then a pocket watch, then a cigarette case, more and more handkerchiefs, until he is at last transformed from a gentleman of minor pretensions into a full-scale dandy.

Fully transformed, Pip enter Jaggers' offices.

Jaggers Mr Pip.

Pip Mr Jaggers.

Jaggers Take a chair.

Enter an Old Woman through the office door.

Old Woman Oh, Mr Jaggers! Take my case, Mr Jaggers!

Jaggers Why are you here, Amelia? Wemmick!

A Young Man also appears at the door.

Young Man Oh, Mr Jaggers, sir . . .

Jaggers I have nothing to say to you, sir. Where is that clerk of mine? Wemmick! (*to Young Man*) I want to know no more than I know. Now both of you out of my sight!

They leave.

Mr Pip. I must call you Mr Pip today. One and twenty, Mr Pip. Congratulations, sir.

Pip Thank you, Mr Jaggers.

Jaggers Take a chair. Now, my young friend, I am going to have a word or two with you.

An Old Man enters, coughing, and splutters an attempt at words.

Now I won't have it! Another word and I throw the case!

Exit the Old Man.

You have been living in this city now for how long?

Pip Four years, sir.

Jaggers Four years, three months, Mr Pip. And what do you suppose you are living at the rate of?

Pip At the rate of, sir?

Jaggers At – the rate of?

Pip I confess I am unable to answer that question, sir.

Jaggers I thought so.

Enter a Jew.

Jew Mr Jaggerth!

Jaggers Who are you? Wemmick, where are you?! (*to the Jew*) Let go of my coat.

Jew Habraham Latharuth. On suspicion of plate.

Jaggers Too late. I am against you.

Jew Don't say it, Mr Jaggers!

Jaggers I am and that's the end of it. Get out of my office!

Jew But Mr Jaggers!

Jaggers Away!

Exit Jew.

Mr Pip, attend if you please. You have been drawing
pretty freely here: your name occurs pretty often in the
cash book; but you are in debt, of course?

Pip I am afraid I must say yes, sir.

Jaggers You know you must say yes, don't you?

Pip Yes, sir.

Jaggers I don't ask what you owe, because you don't
know, and if you did know, you wouldn't tell me; you
would say less. Yes yes, my friend, it's likely enough that
you think you wouldn't, but you would.

Enter Wemmick, the office clerk.

(*not seeing who it is*) Away! (*seeing him*) Ah, Wemmick,
where have you been? We have been under constant
attack.

Wemmick At Newgate, Mr Jaggers. Visiting the
unfortunate and the undeserving. Good day, Mr Pip, sir.
And congratulations. One and twenty!

Pip Thank you, Mr Wemmick.

Jaggers Wemmick, please be so good as to give Mr Pip
this piece of paper. Mr Pip, take the piece of paper in
your hand. Unfold it and tell me what it is.

Pip This is a bank note for five hundred pounds.

Jaggers That is a bank note for five hundred pounds.
A handsome sum of money. You consider it so?

Pip Undoubtedly.

Jaggers Undoubtedly. Now that handsome sum of money, Mr Pip, is your own. It is a present to you, in earnest of your expectations. And at the rate of five hundred pounds per annum, and no higher rate, you are to live until the donor of the whole appears. That is to say, you will now take your money affairs entirely into your own hands.

Pip I am very grateful to my benefactor . . .

Jaggers I am not paid to carry your words to anyone.

Pip But it would be a great relief to me to ask you several questions . . .

Jaggers Such as?

Pip Is my benefactor to be made known to me today?

Jaggers No.

Pip Is that confidence to be imparted to me soon?

Jaggers No.

Pip That evening we first met in my old village, you told me it might be years hence that my patron appeared. It is now four years. Do you suppose it will still be years hence, Mr Jaggers?

Jaggers That's a question that must not be asked.

Pip Ever since my arrival in London I have looked forward to my one and twentieth birthday with a crowd of speculations and anticipations.

Jaggers looks at Wemmick. Wemmick leaves.

Jaggers Come! I'll go a little further with you. I'll say something more. When that person discloses, it will not be necessary for me to know anything about it. Is that clear?

Pip Yes, but . . .

Jaggers Wemmick will see you out.

Exit Jaggers. Wemmick re-enters.

Wemmick One and twenty, Mr Pip.

Pip Yes, Mr Wemmick.

Wemmick Speaking in a private and personal capacity, Mr Pip, if I may, I remember when you first arrived in this office, like a boy, sir, like a small boy. And now what, sir?

Pip What Wemmick?

Wemmick Why, sir . . . in a private and personal capacity . . . A gentleman, sir. A gentleman!

TWO

The Finches gentlemen's club. Pip and several other young men (including Bentley Drummle), in formal evening wear, are toasting themselves gaily.

1st Finch Gentlemen, may the present promotion of good feeling ever reign predominant among the Finches of the Grove!

Finches The Finches of the Grove!

The young men swallow their glasses in one, slam them down and start to chant in unison.

The pledges! The pledges! The pledges!

A Finch stands drunkenly to great cheers, taps the table three times, makes a rather strange movement as if he is rustling his feathers and speaks . . .

1st Finch It behoves me, gentlemen, Finches of the Grove, in accordance with our great tradition, to request you all to raise your glasses in praise of the unparalleled beauty of my lady of pledge: Lady Amelia Bulstrode!

Finches Lady Amelia Bulstrode!

2nd Finch (*standing just like the first*) It is called upon me, gentlemen of the Grove, in accordance with Finch tradition, to second the honourable gentleman's commendation of his lady Miss Bulstrode, only to temper it with higher praise still for the angelic countenance of my lady of pledge: Miss Sarah Forringe!

Finches Miss Sarah Forringe!

3rd Finch (*standing like the other two, but very drunk*) It is my solemn duty . . . in the great traditition of Finchdom, to honour the beauteous beauteousness of the aforementioned Bulstrode and Forringe only to subjubjugate that praise in favour of the eminent and copious allure of my lady of pledge: Miss Emily DuCann!

Finches Miss Emily DuCann!

1st Finch Sir. Whilst declaring you a true Finch and honourable gentleman in your fulfilling of your duty in the honouring of the allure of Miss DuCann, I declare you, sir, a blackguard, sir, for the slight placed upon the beauty of my lady of pledge: Miss Amelia Bulstrode.

2nd Finch And you, sir, I lay the glove of offence at your door, sir, for the insult to Miss Sarah Forringe, whose loveliness o'ershadows the allure of Miss DuCann as an eagle soaring above a lowly osprey.

3rd Finch An osprey, sir? You refer to my lady of pledge as an osprey!

1st Finch An osprey, sir! For so she is!

1st Finch If your Forringe, sir, is an eagle o'ershadowing an osprey, then my Bulstrode, sir, is an angel, sir, that casts your Bulstrode into darkest shadow.

1st Finch You that say that, sir, are a scoundrel, sir.

3rd Finch And you that say that, sir, are a rascal, sir!

1st Finch And you, sir, and you, sir, are scoundrels and rascals both, sirs!

1st Finch I demand satisfaction of you, sir!

3rd Finch And I of you, sir!

1st Finch And I of you, sir! And of you, sir!

1st Finch And of you, sir!

3rd Finch And of you, sir!

A three-way fight ensues until another Finch stands on the table. He is Bentley Drummle.

4th Finch Stand down for Bentley Drummle! Stand down for Mr Bentley Drummle.

Finches Drummle! Drummle!

Drummle Gentlemen! Finches of the Grove! You forget the strict decorum of the Finchian pledge. There shall be no debate nor duel nor debacle until all the pledges have been heard. And we have not heard our youngest Finch's pledge to his fair lady.

Finches Hear hear! Well said, Drummle!

Drummle Come then, Mr Pip! Who is your lady, sir? Speak! Or have you no lady sir to speak of?

Finches Ha ha ha!

Pip As a man who only this morning was found lying head down in a drain, Mr Drummle is feeling remarkably sprightly this evening.

Drummle Gentlemen, Mr Pip's stubbornness leads us, against our will, to assume the worst. Mr Pip is a ladyless lily-liver!

Finches Ha ha ha!

Pip (*raises his glass*) Mr Drummle, gentlemen, fellow Finches, as I have come of age just this week, I have not before this date had the Grove's honourable permission to pledge my allegiance to any lady. But be assured that a lady there is, one who though not yet mine due to her studying abroad these last four years, is destined for me by a higher power. One whose loveliness would dazzle each and every one of your ladies as the sun blinds even the most radiant angel. I call upon the assembled company to salute and honour a paragon, a miracle in woman's form, my lady of pledge – Miss Estella of Satis!

Finches Miss Estella of Satis!

> *They lift Pip up in triumph, crying out in wild drunken joy.*

Miss Estella of Satis!

> *And there Estella is, beckoning Pip, but as they carry him closer so they sweep him away further like a wave never quite reaching the certainty of the shore . . .*

THREE

A letter from Biddy.

Biddy My dear Mr Pip. I write this by request of Mr Gargery for to let you know that he is going to London and would be glad if agreeable to see you. We talk of you in the kitchen every night, and wonder what you are saying and doing. If now considered in the light of a liberty, excuse it for the love of poor old days. No more, dear Mr Pip. Your ever obliged and affectionate servant. Biddy.

P.S. He wishes most particular to write what larks. He says you will understand. He wishes me most particular to write again what larks.

Pip stands silently in his smart London lodgings.

Pip If I could pay to keep him away, I would.

Enter Joe, in absurd town clothes, wiping his feet endlessly.

Joe. How are you, Joe?

Joe Pip. How air you, Pip?

Pip I'm glad to see you, Joe. Give me your hat.

But Joe won't, hanging on to it. Pause.

Joe Which you have that growed and that swelled and that gentlefolked as to be sure you are an honour to your king and country.

Pip And you look wonderfully well.

Joe Thank God I'm ekerval to most. And these are your rooms . . .

Joe looks around the room.

They're not as large now as I'd imagined.

Pip When did you come to town?

Joe Were it yesterday afternoon? No, it were not. Yes, it were. It were yesterday afternoon.

Pip Why don't you sit down, Joe?

Joe (*not sitting. Pause*) Us two being alone, sir . . .

Pip Joe, how can you call me sir?

Joe Us two being now alone, and me having the intentions and abilities to stay not many minutes more, I will now conclude – leastways begin to mention – what have led to my having had the present honour. Well, sir, this is how it were. I were in the Bargemen the other night when there comes up in his shay cart, Pumblechook. And his word were: Joseph, Miss Havisham she wish to speak to you.

Pip Miss Havisham? Go on, please.

Joe Next day, sir, having cleaned myself I go and see Miss A. Her expression air as following. Mr Gargery, you are in correspondence with Mr Pip. Having had more than a letter from you, I were able to say I am. Would you tell him then, said she, that which Estella has come home and would be glad to see him.

Pause.

Pip Estella is back? When? Where is she?

Joe Biddy, when I got home, says I know he will be glad to have the message word of mouth, it is holiday-time, you want to see him, go! I have concluded, sir, and Pip, I wish you ever well and ever prospering to a greater and greater height.

Pause.

Pip You're going now?

Joe Yes, I am.

Pip But you are coming back for dinner?

Joe No, I am not.

Pip But Joe!

Joe Pip, dear chap, life is made of so many partings welded together, as I may say. Divisions among men must come and must be met as they come. If there's ben any fault today's it's mine in coming. You and me is not two figures to be together in London. It ain't that I'm proud, but that I want to be right. I'm wrong in these clothes. You won't find half so much fault in me if you think of me in my forge dress with my hammer in my hand and my pipe in my mouth. And so God bless you, dear old Pip, old chap, God bless you!

He touches him gently on the forehead and leaves. Pip pauses then grabs his hat.

Pip Estella! At last our time has come!

FOUR

Miss Havisham's. Miss Havisham enters in a wheelchair, wheeled in by an elegant young woman. Pip kisses Miss Havisham's hand.

Miss Havisham So, after all this time, you still kiss my hand as if I were a queen eh? – Well?

Pip looks up at the woman. Yes, it is Estella. Estella gives Pip her hand.

Pip Estella. It is you.

Miss Havisham Do you find her much changed, Pip?

Pip When I came in, I thought there was nothing of Estella in the face and figure, but now it all settles down so curiously into the old –

Miss Havisham You're not going to say the old Estella? She was proud and insulting and you wanted to go away from her, don't you remember?

Pip That was long ago.

Miss Havisham Is he changed?

Estella Very much.

Miss Havisham Less coarse and common?

Estella laughs. Pip laughs.

Estella is to come to London. You must introduce her to your society, Mr Pip.

Pip I look forward greatly to that occasion.

Estella Since your change of fortune and prospects, you have changed your companions.

Pip Naturally.

Estella And necessarily, what was fit company for you once would be quite unfit company for you now.

Pip From my life before, I can truly say, I see no one.

Miss Havisham I wish to speak with Pip alone for a minute. Then he will join you in the courtyard.

Estella leaves.

Miss Havisham Is she beautiful, graceful, well grown? Do you admire her?

Pip Everybody who sees her, must.

Miss Havisham Love her, love her, love her! If she wounds you, love her! If she tears your heart to pieces – and as it gets older and stronger, it will tear deeper – love her love her love her! I adopted her to be loved. I bred her and educated her to be loved. I developed her into what she is, that she might be loved! I'll tell you what real love is. It is blind devotion, unquestioning self-humiliation, utter submission, trust and belief against yourself and against the whole world, giving up your heart and soul to the smiter – as I did!

Miss Havisham rises from her chair in fury, and Pip catches her as she almost faints, exhausted.

Love her love her love her!

Enter Estella. Miss Havisham fades into the darkness. Pause.

Estella How do I appear to you?

Pip As even more beautiful than when you left.

Pause.

I watched you here the first day I came. You walked on the casks.

Estella Did I?

Pip And you gave me my food to eat like a dog.

Estella I don't remember.

Pip Not remember that you made me cry?

Estella You must know that I have no heart. If that has anything to do with my memory.

Pip I hope you will not take offence if I doubt that very much.

Estella Oh, I have a heart to be stabbed in or shot in, I have no doubt, and of course if it ceased to beat I should cease to be. But you know what I mean: I have no softness – no sympathy – sentiment – nonsense.

Pip Estella . . .

Estella I am serious. If we are to be thrown much together, you had better believe it at once.

Pip But Estella . . .

Estella No. I have not bestowed my tenderness anywhere. I have never had any such thing.

Pause.

Pip Where will you stay in London?

Estella I am going to Richmond. Our lesson is that there are two Richmonds, one in Surrey and one in Yorkshire, and that mine is the Surrey Richmond. I am going to live at a great expense with a lady who has the power – or says she has – of taking me about and showing me to people.

Pip I suppose you will be glad of the admiration.

Estella I suppose I will.

Pip You speak of yourself as if you were someone else.

Estella Where did you learn how I speak of others? Come, come. I must talk in my own way. How do you thrive in your lodgings?

Pip I live quite pleasantly there. At least . . .

Estella At least?

Pip As pleasantly as I could anywhere away from you.

Estella You silly boy. How could you talk such nonsense?

Miss Havisham (*suddenly appearing, but not there*) Love her! Love her! Love her!

Pip kisses her hand suddenly.

Estella You ridiculous boy. Will you never take warning? Or do you kiss my hand in the spirit in which I once let you kiss my cheek?

Pip What spirit was that?

Estella I must think a minute. A spirit of contempt for the fawners and plotters.

Pip If I say yes, may I kiss the cheek again?

Estella You should have asked before you touched the hand. But yes, if you like.

> *He does so, with such delicacy and gentleness . . . and as soon as he touches her skin . . .*

Now. You are to take care that a carriage is called and that I get to Richmond.

> *Pip tears away from her in frustration.*

Pip Your reverting to this intercourse gives me pain. Everything you do gives me pain.

Estella (*exactly as before*) You are to take care that a carriage is called and that I get to Richmond.

Pip Whatever your tone, I cannot trust in it and build no hope on it, and yet I go on against trust and against hope.

Miss Havisham Love her! Love her! Love her!

Pip I love her! I love her! I love her!

FIVE

The funeral of Mrs Joe. A coffin is carried across the stage by Joe, Pumblechook and another townsman. They await Pip to join . . .

Pip (*reading a letter in his lodgings*) 'We beg to inform you that Mrs J. Gargery has departed this life on Monday last. Your attendance is requested at the interment on Monday next at three o'clock in the afternoon. Yours, Trabb and Company.'

Pip joins the pall-bearers as Mr Trabb, the undertaker, appears.

Trabb Pocket handkerchiefs out, everyone!

They all take out their handkerchiefs and hold them to their noses and begin to walk, Trabb leading ostentatiously. They enter the graveyard and the coffin is lowered into an open grave in the graveyard. The funeral service continues silently behind. But breaking away . . . Pip suddenly sees a shadow loom over the gravestone of his parents. It looms larger and larger and Pip flees screaming . . .

Biddy Pip?

Pip Biddy!

Biddy Sit down, Pip. You're tired. You haven't been yourself since you got here.

Pip does not sit down. Pause. He looks back to the grave, but the shadow is gone.

Pip Biddy, I think you might have written to me yourself about these sad matters.

Biddy Do you, Mr Pip? I should have written if you thought that.

Pip Don't consider me unkind, Biddy, when I say that you ought to have done that.

Biddy Do you, Mr Pip?

Pip I suppose it will be difficult for you to remain here now.

Biddy Oh, I can't do so, Mr Pip. Though I hope I shall be able to take some care of Mr Gargery until he settles down.

Pip How are you going to live? If you want any money –

Biddy How will I live? I am going to try to get the place of mistress in the new school. The new schools are not like the old but I learnt a good deal from you and have had time since then to improve.

Pip I think you would always improve, Biddy, under any circumstances.

Biddy Ah. Except in my bad side of human nature.

Pip Biddy, I shall be down here often now. I am not going to leave poor Joe alone.

   Pause.

Biddy, don't you hear me?

Biddy Yes, Mr Pip.

Pip Not to mention you calling me Mr Pip, which appears to be in bad taste, Biddy – what do you mean?

Biddy What do I mean?

Pip Biddy, I must request to know what you mean by this!

Biddy By this?

Pip Don't echo! I made a remark respecting my coming down here often to see Joe which you greeted with a marked silence. Have the goodness to tell me why.

Biddy Are you quite sure you will come to see him often?

Pip Oh dear me. This really is a bad side of human nature. Don't say any more if you please, Biddy. This shocks me very much.

Enter Joe in black.

Goodbye, dear, Joe – no, don't wipe it off! – for God's sake – give me your blackened hand! I shall be down soon and often.

Joe Never too soon, sir. And never too often, Pip.

They hug each other. Then he bids farewell to Biddy.

Pip Biddy, I am not angry, but I am hurt.

Biddy No, don't be hurt. Let only me be hurt if I have been ungenerous.

Pip I shall be down here soon, and often. Soon and often!

SIX

Enter Estella. Pip's gaze is immediately distracted from Joe and Biddy, who seem to disappear into the marsh mists . . . We are in Richmond at a fine table. Servants bring tea.

Estella Do you take milk?

Pip Yes, thank you.

Estella And sugar?

Pip No, thank you. And how are you finding Richmond?

Estella I don't know. How does anyone find it?

She hands him his cup. Their hands almost meet.

Pip, why will you never take warning?

Pip Of what?

Estella Of me.

Pip Warning not to be attracted to you, do you mean?

Estella Do I mean! If you don't know what I mean, you are blind.

Pip Love is commonly reputed blind. (*Beat.*) But I consider it ungenerous to press myself upon you, when neither of us can know what others' intentions are for us. And when our suspicion of those intentions necessarily makes us, or one of us, rebellious against them.

Estella I'm sure I don't understand what you mean.

Pip You deny the struggle within your bosom, Estella? You still deny it?

Estella This tea is tepid.

Pip At any rate, I have no warning given me just now, for you wrote to me to come to you this time.

Estella That's true. The time has come round when Miss Havisham wishes to have me for a day at Satis. You are to take me there and bring me back, if you will. Can you take me?

Pip Can I take you! I can and must obey!

Miss Havisham Estella!

Miss Havisham wheels her way to Estella to fawn on her and clutch her hands, hugging her, hanging off her. Pip attends.

I received your letters. I want to know more.

Estella What do you wish to know?

Miss Havisham I want to know of the society you keep. What men court you? What men woo you with their words and gifts?

Estella I have written it all down in the letters I sent you. I will read the letters aloud should you so desire.

Miss Havisham And they admire you?

Estella Some do, I suppose.

Miss Havisham And fawn upon you? And would love you if you would let them near you? Are these men wealthy?

Estella Mostly they are.

Miss Havisham And young?

Estella They are young.

Miss Havisham Name them. I said name them!

Estella In the letters . . .

Miss Havisham I want you to say them! I want you to say their names in front of him!

Estella extracts her hand.

What? Are you grown tired of me?

Estella Only a little tired of myself.

Miss Havisham Speak the truth, you ingrate! You stock and stone! You cold, cold heart!

Estella What? Do you reproach me for being cold? You?

Miss Havisham Are you not?

Estella You should know. I am what you made me. Take all the praise, take all the blame, take all the success and failure. In short, take me.

Miss Havisham Oh, look at her, Pip! Look at her! So hard and thankless on the hearth where she was reared! Where I took her into this wretched breast when it was first bleeding from its stabs and where I have lavished years of tenderness upon her!

Estella At least I was no party to the compact, for if I could walk and speak when it was made, it was as much as I could do. But what would you have? You have been very good to me, and I owe everything to you. What would you have?

Miss Havisham Love.

Estella You have it.

Miss Havisham I have it not!

Estella Mother by adoption, I have said I owe everything to you. All I possess is yours. All that you have given me is at your command to have again. Beyond that I have nothing. And if you ask me to give what you never gave me, my gratitude and duty cannot do impossibilities.

Miss Havisham Did I never give her love, Pip? Did I never give her burning love? Let her call me mad! Let her call me mad!

Estella Why should I call you mad? I of all people. Does anyone live who knows what set purposes you have as well as I do? I who have sat on this same hearth on the little stool that is even now beside you there, learning your lessons and looking into your face, when your face was strange and frightened me!

Miss Havisham Times soon forgotten!

Estella Not forgotten! Not forgotten, but treasured up in my memory. When have you found me false to your teaching? When have you found me unmindful of your lessons? When have you found me giving admission here to anything that you excluded? Be just to me.

Miss Havisham So proud, Pip! So proud!

Estella Who taught me to be proud? Who praised me when I learnt my lesson?

Miss Havisham But to be proud and hard to me. Estella, Estella, Estella, to be proud to me!

Pause.

Pip I think I shall take a walk in the yard.

He walks outside. Miss Havisham and Estella speak to him in his dream.

Miss Havisham I'll tell you what real love is.

Estella You must know that I have no heart.

Miss Havisham It is blind devotion, unquestioning, self-humiliation.

Estella Oh, I have a heart to be stabbed in or shot in . . .

Miss Havisham Trust and belief against yourself and against the whole world.

Estella But you know what I mean. I have no softness . . .

Miss Havisham Giving up your heart and soul to the smiter!

Estella . . . no sympathy – sentiment – nonsense. No!

Miss Havisham As I did!

Estella I have not bestowed my tenderness anywhere.

Miss Havisham As I did!

Estella I have never had any such thing!

SEVEN

The Finches. A sudden invasion of very drunk men. Members of the Finch Club in full flow, very drunk, a very drunk Pip and Bentley Drummle in their company.

1st Finch Finches of the Grove – I call upon the assembled company to raise their glasses and bow before the glory of my jewel, my ruby, my lady of pledge: Miss Prunella Smillitt of Hampstead!

Finches Miss Prunella Smillitt of Hampstead!

2nd Finch And I – I ask you, friends, esteemed Finches, in the great tradition of the Grove – to raise your glasses, and salute the delicate frame and ivory skin of Miss Smillitt as inferior only to that of my Aphrodite, my Venus, my Ophelia! – Miss Jane Herring of Tunbridge!

Finches Miss Jane Herring of Tunbridge!

1st Finch To you, sir, and to your rendering inferior the pale alabaster of Miss Prunella's brow to the tawny visage of Miss Herring – I say you, sir, are a rascal, sir!

Finches Hear hear!

1st Finch And you, sir, I declare, sir, are a scoundrel and a blackguard, sir!

Finches Hear hear!

3rd Finch Silence, Finches! Silence! As presiding Finch, I now call upon Mr Bentley Drummle to toast his lady of pledge, on his honour be it!

Finches Yes, what about you, Drummle!

Pip (*very drunk*) Yes, come on, Drummle, you haven't pledged to a lady since I've been here! Or perhaps there is no lady to pledge!

Much Finchian laughter and yelling of 'Drummle,
Drummle!' Drummle stands and waves for silence.

Drummle Gentlemen, it is true that I have been scant of
compliment as of late. But this abstinence should only
whet your appetites for the delicacy I am to present before
you tonight. It is my profound privilege, gentlemen, to
stand before you and pledge allegiance to a constellation
that outsparkles even the lustre of such a rare gem as
Miss Prunella Smillitt and renders dim even the emerald
eyes of Miss Jane Herring. I call upon you, gentlemen of
the Grove, to raise your glasses – perhaps Mr Pip would
lead the way . . .

Pip Gladly, Mr Drummle. Gladly!

Drummle And to join me in my pledge to the incarnation
of the feminine – Miss Estella of Richmond!

Finches Miss Estella of Richmond!

Pause.

Pip Miss Estella who?

Drummle Never you mind!

Pip But I know that lady.

Drummle Do you?

Pip You know I do! I toasted her not three months ago!

Drummle Did you? Oh *Lord*!

Pip And I can say with some sureness that you have
come down to the Grove bearing the name of a lady of
whom you know nothing!

Drummle I demand to know what you mean by that, sir.

Pip I mean, sir, that you are a liar!

Drummle You will apologise for that slight, sir, or face the sternest rebuke.

Pip I will not apologise, sir! And if you desire satisfaction, sir, you know where I am to be found!

Drummle I do desire satisfaction, sir!

Pip Then unless you can prove, sir, by evidence in the own lady's hand, that you know the lady, I shall await your arrival by the dawn chorus!

Drummle Then, sir, you shall not have need to rise so early, for I have the proof you desire with me on the present occasion! (*He takes out a letter and brandishes it.*) Read it to the assembled company, Mr Pip, and deny that it is her hand!

1st Finch Read the letter, Mr Pip. And if the letter proves true, Mr Drummle and the assembled company shall require a public and abject apology.

Finches Read it! Read it!

Pip (*reading*) 'Dear Mr Drummle, may I thank you for escorting me yesterday evening – I greatly enjoyed our dancing together and look forward to a similar opportunity on another occasion. Yours as ever, Estella.'

Drummle Is it in her hand, sir?

Pip It is in her hand.

Drummle Then I demand a public and abject apology, sir!

Finches Recite the abject apology!

1st Finch (*standing and rustling his feathers, before orating grandly*) I, Mr Pip of the Grove, apologise unreservedly to Mr Drummle . . .

Pip I, Mr Pip of the Grove, apologise unreservedly to Mr Drummle . . .

1st Finch . . . for having doubted his word of honour . . .

Pip . . . for having doubted his word of honour . . .

1st Finch . . . and for having been betrayed into a warmth of passion unbefitting a Finch.

Pip . . . and for having been betrayed into a warmth of passion unbefitting a Finch.

1st Finch I am no longer to be found should he demand satisfaction.

Pip I am no longer to be found should he demand satisfaction.

1st Finch I am no longer to be found anywhere.

Pip I am no longer to be found anywhere.

1st Finch I am a shame to the name of gentleman.

Pip I am a shame to the name of gentleman.

1st Finch After all, nothing but a coarse and common labouring boy.

Pip After all, nothing but a coarse and common labouring boy.

1st Finch A thing of darkness.

Pip A thing of darkness.

1st Finch Undeserving of Estella's love.

Pip Undeserving of Estella's love.

1st Finch Fit only for the forge.

Pip Fit only for the forge.

Finches Hear hear! Hear hear!

Estella appears with a dog's bowl once more, and lays it at his feet. Cheered on by the multitude of Finches, Pip goes on his knees and like a wild dog devours his gruel as Estella leads the Finches in a rousing chorus of 'Old Clem' . . .

EIGHT

Night. Pip alone in his rooms, drunk, in despair. Figures haunt him in his fever.

Pip
Hammer boys around. Old Clem!

Joe Soon and often, Pip! Soon and often!

Pip
With a thump and a sound. Old Clem!

Biddy A bad side of human nature!

Pip
Blow the fire, blow the fire. Old Clem!

Miss Havisham Break their hearts!

Pip
Roaring dryer, soaring higher. Old Clem!

Estella Greatly enjoyed our dancing together . . .

Pip
Beat it out, beat it out. Old Clem!

Drummle Is it her hand? Is it her hand?

Pip
Beat it out, beat it out, old Clem!

The ghosts begin to make a knocking noise, and then as the noise continues, they go silent but remain in the room. Now the knocking, in the darkness, is clearly coming from beneath . . . Pip stops dead.

Who is it? Who is down there? There is someone down there, is there not?

Man's Voice Yes.

Pip What floor do you want?

Man's Voice The top. Mr Pip's rooms.

Pip Then come up! Come up!

A shadow ascends as if from the grave to Pip's level.

Who are you?

A man of sixty. Long grey hair, muscular, hardened by exposure to weather. Heavy, rough clothes. He slightly resembles a disinterred corpse. He holds out his hands to Pip. It is Magwitch, but Pip does not recognise him.

What is your business?

Magwitch My business. Ah yes, I will explain my business, by your leave.

Pip Do you wish to come in?

Magwitch Yes, I wish to come in, master.

He climbs up and holds out both hands to Pip again but Pip keeps his distance.

Pip What do you mean by this?

Magwitch It's disappointing to a man arter having look'd forard so distant, and come so fur; but you're not to blame for that – neither on us is to blame for that. I'll speak in half a minute; give me half a minute, please.

Pause.

There's no one nigh, is there?

Pip Why do you, a stranger coming into my rooms at this time of night, ask that question?

Magwitch You're a game one. I'm glad you grown up a game one. But don't catch hold of me. You'd be sorry arterwards to have done it.

Magwitch holds out his huge hands and shows them in the old gesture. Pip's gesture on the marshes. Pip stares in horror.

Pip I know you. I know who you are.

Magwitch smiles and again holds out his hands. Pip reluctantly gives them to him.

Magwitch You acted noble, my boy. Noble, Pip. And I have never forgot it.

Magwitch moves to embrace Pip, but Pip pushes him away.

Pip Stay! Keep off! If you are grateful to me for what I did when I was a little child, I hope you have shown your gratitude by mending your way of life. If you have come here to thank me, it was not necessary. There may be something good in the feeling that has brought you here, but you must understand that – I –

Pause.

Magwitch You was saying?

Pip That I cannot wish to renew that chance intercourse of long ago, under these different circumstances. I am glad to believe you have repented and recovered yourself. But our ways are different ways, none the less.

Magwitch nods. Pause.

You are wet. You look weary. Will you drink something before you go?

Magwitch I think I will drink, I thank you, before I go.

Magwitch is drinking.

Pip How are you living?

Magwitch I've been a sheepfarmer, stockbreeder, other trades besides, away in the new world. Many a thousand mile of stormy water off from this.

Pip I hope you have done well.

Magwitch I've done wonderful well. There's others went out alonger me as has done well too, but no man has done nigh as well as me. I'm famous for it.

Pip I am glad to hear it.

Magwitch I hope to hear you say so, boy. May I make so bold as ask how you have done well, since you and me was out on them lone shivering marshes?

Pip How?

Magwitch Ah!

Pause.

Pip I have been chosen to . . . succeed to some property.

Magwitch Might a mere warmint ask what property?

Pip I don't know.

Magwitch Might a mere warmint ask whose property?

Pip I don't know.

Magwitch Could I make a guess, I wonder, at your income since you first came of age? As to the figure now . . . Five? Concerning a guardian – there ought to be some guardian – whiles you was a minor. Some lawyer maybe? As to the first letter of that name? Would it be J? Might it be Jaggers?

Pause.

Pip Oh no. Oh God, no.

Magwitch Oh yes, Pip, dear boy, I've made a gentleman of you. It's me wot has done it! I swore at that time, sure as ever I earned a guinea, that guinea should go to you. I swore arterwards, sure as ever I spec'lated and got rich, you should get rich. I lived rough that you should live smooth. I worked hard, that you should be above work. Do I tell it fur you to feel a obligation? Not a bit. I tell it fur you to know as that there hunted dunghill dog wot you kep life in got his head so high that he could make a gentleman – and Pip – you're him! Why, look at you, dear boy! Look at these here lodgings of yours, fit for a lord! Look at your clothes. (*taking a watch from Pip's pocket*) Lookee 'ere. A gold'un and a beauty! That's a gentleman's! A diamond set around with rubies. That's a gentleman's! Look at your linen. And your books too, mounting up on the shelves by hundreds. And you read 'em, don't you? I bet you'd been a reading them when I came in. You shall read 'em to me, dear boy! Like a son! You're my son – more to me nor any son! You're mine!

Pause.

But didn't you ever think it might be me?

Pip Oh no no no. Never!

Magwitch Well, you see it was. Not a soul in it but me.

Pip Was there no one else?

Magwitch Who else should there be?

Pause.

Where will you put me?

Pip What?

Magwitch I must be put somewheres, dear boy.

Pip Here?

Magwitch Yes, and to sleep long and sound, for I've been sea-tossed and sea-washed months and months. Is there a back room?

Pip Yes.

Magwitch Thankee, boy. And boy. No one will come tomorrow? Because caution is necessary.

Pip What do you mean?

Magwitch By God. It's death!

Pip What's death?

Magwitch I was sent there for life. It's death to come back. If I be took, I should of a certainty be hang'd.

Pip No one will come!

Magwitch Good night, boy.

He hugs him again. And leaves. Pip, half-drunk, exhausted, is left alone.

Pip What do I do? What do I do? Throw him out! Give him up! I cannot. He is as much a part of me as I myself. And he will tell people. He will cut me off. I will have to go back to the forge, Estella will hear of it, all will be lost. No no no! I could flee. Go abroad where no man can find me. Give up everything? Give up all hope of

316

her? I cannot. I cannot! Oh how can I seal those lips for ever so no one will know? How?

Pip sits in his chair. Night turns to morning. Magwitch, dressed more as a gentleman, is slicing bread with a knife.

Magwitch This is good thick bread arter having journeyed so long on scraps.

Pip approaches him, takes the knife and looks at it. Magwitch is eating oblivious. Pip stares at the knife, then at Magwitch. He begins to raise the knife over Magwitch's head and is about to cut the old man's throat . . . A fight takes place – terrible and violent – to the death – but it all ends just as they were – over breakfast, Magwitch slicing the bread as before.

This is good thick bread arter having journeyed so long on scraps.

Pause.

Pip I have given out amongst the watchmen that you are my uncle.

Magwitch That's it, dear boy. Call me Uncle.

Pip But you must bear the clothes I have given you with more grace.

Magwitch The hut-life is in me now, boy. I won't be tamed now.

Pip But you have to be! I cannot be seen with you holding that savage air. People will talk, they will load you with all the crimes in the *Calendar* and we will both be shunned by society. We have to create you anew. As if you were quite another person from what you are.

Magwitch As you wish, dear boy.

Pip You assumed some name I suppose on board ship?

Magwitch I took the name of Provis.

Pip Do you mean to keep that name?

Magwitch Unless you'd like another.

Pip What is your real name?

Magwitch Magwitch. Christen'd Abel. (*Magwitch takes out a pocketbook and throws it on the table.*) There's something worth spending in that there book, dear boy. It's yourn. All I've got ain't mine. It's yourn. I've come to the old country fur to see my gentleman spend his money like a gentleman. That'll be my pleasure! And blast you all! Blast you every one, from the judge in his wig to the colonist stirring up dust, I'll show you a better gentleman than the whole kit on you put together!

Pip Stop!! Stop, for God's sake! I want to speak to you! I want to know what is to be done. I want to know how you are to be kept out of danger, how you are to be kept secret . . .

Magwitch If the danger had been fifty times as great, I should still ha' come to see you, Pip.

    Pause.

Pip (*to Magwitch*) Stay inside. I will return tomorrow. And don't go out until I do so.

Magwitch Where are you going, boy?

Pip Stay inside!

Magwitch Where are you going?

NINE

Miss Havisham's room. Estella pushes Miss Havisham.

Miss Havisham What wind blows you here, Pip?

Pip I have something to say to Estella, Miss Havisham, and what I have to say I will say before you. It will not surprise you, it will not displease you. I am as unhappy as you can ever have meant me to be. I have found out who my patron is. It is not a fortunate discovery, and is not likely ever to enrich me in reputation, station, fortune, anything.

Miss Havisham Well?

Pip When you first caused me to be brought here, Miss Havisham, when I belonged to the village over yonder, that I wish I had never left; I suppose I did really come here as any other chance boy might have come – as a kind of servant, to gratify a want or a whim and to be paid for it?

Miss Havisham Ay, Pip. You did.

Pip And that Mr Jaggers . . .

Miss Havisham Mr Jaggers had nothing to do with it, and knew nothing of it.

Pip But when I fell into the mistake I have so long remained in, at least you led me on?

Miss Havisham Yes. I led you on.

Pip Was that kind?

Miss Havisham (*with sudden fury*) Who am I? Who am I, for God's sake, that I should be kind! (*Pause.*) What else?

Pip What else I have to say is to Estella. Estella, you know I love you. You know that I have loved you long and dearly. I should have said this sooner, but for my long mistake. It induced me to hope that Miss Havisham meant us for one another. But I must say it now!

Estella shakes her head.

I know! I know I have no hope and that I shall never call you mine! Still, I love you! I have loved you ever since I first saw you in this house!

Estella It seems that there are sentiments, fancies – I don't know how to call them – which I am not able to comprehend. When you say you love me, I know what you mean, as a form of words; but nothing more. You address nothing in my breast, you touch nothing there. I have tried to warn you of this, have I not?

Pip Yes.

Estella But you would not be warned, for you thought I did not mean it. Did you not think so?

Pip I thought and hoped you could not mean it. You were so young, untried and beautiful, Estella! Surely it is not in nature!

Estella It is in my nature! It is in the nature formed within me. I make great difference between you and all other people when I say so much. I can do no more.

Pip Is it true that Bentley Drummle is in town and is pursuing you?

Estella It is quite true.

Pip That you encourage him and ride out with him, and that he dines with you this very day?

Estella Quite true.

Pip You cannot love him, Estella!

Estella What have I told you? Do you still think, in spite of it, that I do not mean what I say?

Pip But you would never . . . marry him?

Pause.

Estella Why not tell you the truth? I am going to be married to him.

Pip No!! Estella, dearest, dearest Estella, do not let Miss Havisham lead you into this fateful step. Put me aside for ever – you have done so, I well know, but bestow yourself on some worthier person than Drummle.

Estella I am going to be married to Drummle. And I shall marry him soon. It is my own act!

Pip Your own act to fling yourself away on a brute!

Estella On whom should I fling myself away? Miss Havisham would have me wait, but I am tired. Tired of the life I led, which has very few charms for me, and I am willing enough to change it. There! It is done. Say no more. We shall never understand each other.

Pip Such a mean brute! Such a stupid brute!

Estella Don't be afraid of my being a blessing to him. I shall not be that. Come! Here is my hand. Do we part on this, you visionary boy – or man?

Pip Oh Estella, how can I see you Drummle's wife!

Estella Nonsense. This will pass in no time.

Pip Never, Estella!

Estella You will get me out of your thoughts in a week.

Pip Out of my thoughts! You are part of my existence, part of myself. You have been in every line I have ever read, since I first came here. You have been in every prospect I have ever seen, on the river, on the sails of ships, on the marshes, in the clouds, in the lights, in the darkness, in the wind, in the woods, in the sea, in the streets. You have been the embodiment of every graceful fancy that my mind has ever become acquainted with. The stones of which the strongest London buildings are made are not more real that your presence and influence have been to me, there and everywhere, and will be, Estella, to the last hour of my life. You cannot choose but remain part of my character, part of the little good in me, part of the evil. God bless you, God forgive you.

> *Pip holds her hand to his lips and holds it there for a few lingering moments.*

Estella I must leave now.

Pip Where are you going?

Estella I am meeting my future husband. Goodbye, Pip.

> *Estella leaves. Miss Havisham stares on in ghastly horror. Pause.*

Pip I may as well tell you that this will be the last time we see each other.

Miss Havisham Perhaps you can never believe now that there is anything human in my heart.

Pip I believe that, if anything, your heart is too human.

Miss Havisham Are you very unhappy now?

Pip I . . . I . . . am far from happy, Miss Havisham, but I have other causes for disquiet than any you would know. There are reasons why I must say no more.

Miss Havisham It is noble in you to tell me that you have other causes of unhappiness. Is it true?

Pip Too true.

Miss Havisham Is there nothing I can do for you?

Pip Nothing.

Miss Havisham Oh, what have I done? What have I done?

Pip If you mean, what have you done to injure me, let me answer. Very little. I should have loved her under any circumstances.

Miss Havisham Until you spoke to her as you did, until I saw in you a looking-glass that showed me what I once felt myself, I did not know . . . What have I done?

Pip Miss Havisham, listen to me. You may dismiss me from your mind and conscience. But Estella is a different case, and if you can ever undo any scrap of what you have done amiss in keeping a part of her right nature away from her, it will be better to do that than to bemoan the past through a hundred years.

Miss Havisham But Pip – my dear! My dear! Believe this. When she first came to me, I meant to save her from a misery like my own. But as she grew and promised to be very beautiful, I gradually did worse and with my praises, and with my jewels, and with my teachings, and with this figure of myself always before her as a warning to back and point my lessons, I stole her heart away and put ice in its place.

Pip Better to have left a natural heart, even to be bruised and broken.

Miss Havisham If you knew all my story, you would have some compassion for me and a better understanding of me!

Pip Your house tells your story like a book. (*Pause.*) Miss Havisham, I have to leave now. And I am unlikely to return.

Miss Havisham Where are you going?

Pip I am not at liberty to tell you.

Miss Havisham But you must come back and visit me.

Pip There is nothing for me here!

Miss Havisham Don't go. You are my hope!

Pip Let me go!

Miss Havisham No! Never! You must stay and whisper in my ear that you forgive me. Every day you must come!

Pip Let me go, Miss Havisham.

He pulls away from her, but she grabs on to him.

Miss Havisham Every night and every day you must come to me and say it! 'I forgive you!'

Miss Havisham rises unsteadily from her chair to chase him.

Pip Miss Havisham, be careful. The fire.

Miss Havisham Say it! 'I forgive you!'

Pip Miss Havisham, the fire!

Miss Havisham Say, 'I forgive you!'

Pip Your dress. It's on fire!

Miss Havisham Say it!

Pip Miss Havisham! The fire! Miss Havisham!

Miss Havisham Say it! Say it! Say it! Aaaah!

Pip tries to beat down the flames but they only grow higher as the woman screams and screams.

'I forgive you! I forgive you! I forgive you!'

Miss Havisham burns up in front of Pip's eyes . . . and falls upon him as she burns.

TEN

A shadow at the bottom of the stairs. Pip arrives at his chambers, his hands bandaged. He is about to climb the stair.

Pip Provis? Is that you?

On the stairs Pip falls over a man. Pip lights a match. He sees the face of the second convict from the marshes, Compeyson, blemish on cheek and all . . .

Aaaah! Provis! Provis!

Compeyson pushes Pip away, holds a knife to his throat, when . . .

Voice Who's there?

Compeyson releases Pip and runs away into the darkness . . . Pip sprints up the stairs to his rooms . . . In the room a shadow sits on the chair.

Pip Provis! Provis!

A light is turned on. It is Wemmick.

Wemmick Halloa, Mr Pip.

Pip Wemmick. Where is . . .?

Wemmick But what has become of your hands?

Pip (*gripping him*) Where is he? What have you done with him?

Wemmick Now, Mr Pip, you know. You and I understand one another. We are in our private and personal capacities.

Pip What of it?

Wemmick I accidentally heard, yesterday morning, in Newgate Prison, that a certain person not altogether of uncolonial pursuits, and not unpossessed of portable property, we won't name this person . . . had made some little stir in a certain part of the world where people go not always in gratification of their own inclination, by disappearing from such a place, from which conjectures had been raised and theories formed. I also heard that you had been watched . . . and this lodging also . . .

Pip By whom?

Wemmick I wouldn't go into that. It might clash with official responsibilities. But what happened to your hands . . .?

Pip Where is he?

Wemmick Now, I come to what I did after hearing what I heard. I came here to find you, but instead I found to my surprise, a certain . . . Tom, Jack or Richard, and took it upon myself to find a temporary tenement for the said person, a small safe house with a bow window by the river, belonging to a friend . . . and so by nine o'clock last night, there he was secretly housed, and here I have been, waiting for you.

Pip Take me to him.

Wemmick Here is the address. I have done the most I can do, in a private and personal capacity. I must now return to my official capacity. And with that I bid you good day. And Mr Pip. Be sure you are not followed. There is grave danger to him if he be caught. Grave danger.

And Wemmick mimes the noose as he leaves.

ELEVEN

The house with the bow window. Magwitch lies alone. A tapping at the door.

Pip Provis?

Magwitch Pip? Pip, my boy!

He opens and Pip enters.

But your hands, my boy! What happened?

Pip I got too close to a flame.

Magwitch Sit down, and I will dress them!

Pip You met Wemmick?

Magwitch In a personal and private capacity, aye, my boy, that I did.

Pip And what did he tell you?

Magwitch That I am being followed.

Pip By who?

Magwitch He wouldn't say, but I knew as much. By the law, and by . . . by . . .

Pip By whom?

Magwitch By Compeyson.

Pip The other man on the marsh.

Magwitch Aye, boy.

Pip Who is he?

Magwitch A gentleman swindler and a forger and a man as got me into such nets as made me his black slave. It was him got me committed for felony – and when we was sentenced it was him that gets seven years and me that gets fourteen, because he was a gentleman. We was put in the same prison ship. Then one night I escape, and I see my boy, and you tells me that he's out there too. And I hunt him down and smash his face. 'And now,' says I, 'as the worst thing I can do, caring nothing for myself, I'll drag you back myself.'

Pip What happened to him?

Magwitch He had much the best of it to the last. I was put in irons, brought to trial again and sent for life. I don't much know what became of him.

Pip Then I must tell you that he was at the bottom of my stair, when I returned this evening.

Magwitch I'll kill him. I'll tear his face from his shoulders!

Pip My dear Provis. Do you not see what this means? He must have received information that you have returned, and his suspicion must be that you are residing with me. And given what you each think one of the other, it would not surpass him to tell what he knows to people we would not wish to be told.

Magwitch Then what do you propose, boy?

Pip You have to leave tomorrow. Be assured, if the law are told you are here, they will come for you.

Magwitch Where will I leave for?

Pip First for Europe. Then maybe beyond.

Magwitch But I have only just returned to see you a gentleman . . . and to enlarge your expenses . . .

Pip What point is there in that, if you are hanged before you see it!

Magwitch Leave you when I have come so far to see you? Never!

Pip You will not be leaving me. I will come with you.

Magwitch You, boy?

Pip We will row a boat downstream until dark, choose a resting place, and at first light slip ourselves on to a steamer heading to Europe and beyond.

Magwitch But your expectations!

Pip You may find this impossible to comprehend, Provis, and I shall not attempt to explain it to you. You will simply have to believe me when I say, I have none.

NINE

The river. A boatman smoking at dawn.

Pip I need a small rowing boat.

Boatman Where you taking her?

Pip I will pay more money for less questions.

The exchange is made and the boat appears. Magwitch enters the boat. Pip follows and they start to row.

Magwitch If you knowed, dear boy, what it is to sit here alonger my dear boy and have my smoke arter having been day and night betwixt four walls, you'd envy me. But you don't know what it is.

Pip If all goes well, you will be free again within a few hours.

Magwitch Well, I hope so.

Pip And think so?

Magwitch Aye, I s'pose so, I think so, dear boy. We'd be puzzled to be more quiet and easy-going than we are at present. But – it's a flowing so soft and pleasant through the water, p'raps, as makes me think it – I was thinking through my smoke just then, that we can no more see the bottom of the next few hours, than we can see to the bottom of this river what I catches hold of. Nor yet we can't hold more tide than I can hold this. And it's run through my fingers and gone, you see.

Magwitch suddenly sits up.

Pip What is it?

Magwitch What was that ripple?

Pip I saw no ripple.

Magwitch A while back. I thought I saw a boat.

Pip It was nothing.

Magwitch The mind, Pip. The mind.

The light begins to fade.

Pip We're reaching marsh country. My country.

Magwitch Where we first became acquainted, boy.

Pip The steamer will be here soon.

The shadow of another boat heaves into view. Two men in the boat: we do not see their faces.

Voice 1 Holloa there!

Pip and Magwitch freeze.

Pip Who's that?

Voice 1 You see a four-oared galley going up with the tide?

Pip No.

Voice 2 (*to Voice 1*) She must have gone down, then.

Voice 1 (*to Voice 2*) Yet she took up too when she left.

Voice 2 (*to Voice 1*) They must ha' thought better on't.

Pip To what are you referring?

Voice 1 A four-oared galley came by here. We was wondering what they was.

Pip I don't know.

Voice 1 (*to Pip*) He thinks they was, what they wasn't.

Voice 2 I know what I thinks.

Pip You think what?

Voice 1 You thinks Customs.

Voice 2 I do.

Voice 1 Then you're wrong.

Voice 2 Am I? A four don't go hanging and hovering up with one tide and down with another without their being Customs at the bottom of it. They're after someone. (*Pause. Leans forward to Pip.*) Unless you know who it was? (*He laughs and the boat disappears into the mist.*)

Pip They've gone. You think it really was Customs? I don't think so. No one followed us. I don't think so.

Magwitch I was just thinking how there's no light as haunting as the dusk over yon marshes. (*He stiffens.*)

331

Pip What is it? What is it?

The sound of a steamer.

(*to Magwitch*) That's the steamer. That's her! Good luck, Provis.

Magwitch And you, boy. And you. Row into her track now.

They row into the track of the steamer.

Pip She's coming! We are free, Provis! We are free!

Magwitch What's that boat shooting out from under the bank?

Pip (*looking*) A four-oared galley. Row, Provis! Row!

A voice comes from the darkness.

Voice You have a returned transport there. That's the man – wrapped in the cloak! His name is Abel Magwitch. I apprehend that man, and call upon him to surrender and you to assist.

Another boat appears. Four silhouettes, one of whom stands, ready to leap on to Pip and Magwitch's boat.

Magwitch Compeyson!

Compeyson leaps on to Magwitch and the two men fight. The sound of the approaching steamer is deafening now. Suddenly both men fall into the water and disappear.
The sound of the steamer overwhelms the scene.

Pip Provis! Provis! Magwitch! Magwitch! Magwitch!

THIRTEEN

Magwitch is in prison, gravely injured, gravely ill. The keys of the cell open the lock and Pip enters, followed by a Jailer.

Magwitch Dear boy. I thought you was late. But I knowed you couldn't be that.

Pip It is just the time. I waited at the gate.

Magwitch You always wait at the gate, don't you, dear boy?

Pip Yes. Not to lose a moment's time.

Magwitch Thankee, boy. Thankee!

   Pause.

Is it tomorrow?

Pip I have written a petition to the Chief Justice to delay the execution. And I have even appealed to the Crown itself. I have spent today walking up and down the streets waiting for a reply.

Magwitch But none came.

Pip None yet. There is still hope.

Magwitch It is tomorrow.

Pip They searched me when I came in today.

Magwitch They thought you was carrying poison for me.

Pip Yes.

Magwitch Why are you crying, boy?

Pip I am so full of grief to think you came back for my sake.

Magwitch Dear boy. I am quite content to have taken my chance. I've seen a boy, and he can be a gentleman without me. (*Pause.*) What is it, boy?

Pip You must know that as a criminal all your possessions will be forfeited to the Crown. I will receive nothing.

Pause.

Magwitch Then you are here . . . just for me? (*Pause.*) You have never deserted me, boy.

Pip I once meant to. I once meant to do much worse than leave you.

Magwitch And what's the best of all, you've been more comfortable alonger me, since I was under a dark cloud, than when the sun shone.

The Jailer rattles the bars of the prison.

Jailer Time.

Magwitch Hold my hand, boy.

Jailer Time.

Magwitch Hold my hand.

Pip Yes, Abel.

Magwitch I . . .

Jailer Time.

The Jailer enters.

Newgate Prison. Magwitch hangs from a rope. Pip stands alone at the base.

Pip O Lord, be merciful to him, a sinner!

FOURTEEN

Pip lies in bed as images from his life haunt him to the chorus of 'Lord be merciful to him, a sinner.' Miss Havisham, Estella, Magwitch, Pumblechook, Drummle, Biddy – all fly by, lifting him and turning him in a wild delirium. 'Lord be merciful to him, a sinner!' Finally the cacophony of images slowly resolves into one image: the gentle face of Joe Gargery, tending Pip at his bedside.

Pip Is it Joe?

Joe Which it air, old chap.

Pip Oh Joe. You break my heart! Look angry at me, Joe. Strike me, Joe. Tell me of my ingratitude. Don't be so good to me!

Joe Which, dear Pip, old chap, you and me was ever friends.

Joe lifts Pip up until he is standing.

Pip How long, dear Joe?

Joe Which you meantersay, Pip, how long have your illness lasted, dear old chap?

Pip Yes, Joe.

Joe It's the end of May, Pip. Tomorrow is the first of June.

Pip And have you been here all the time, dear Joe?

Joe Pretty nigh, old chap. For Biddy's word were, 'Go to him, without loss of time. Without a minute's loss of time!'

Pip Have you heard . . . who my patron was?

Joe I heerd.

Pip Did you hear that he was dead? Did you hear of his circumstances. If you would like to hear . . .?

Joe Lookee 'ere, old chap. Ever the best of friends, ain't us, Pip? Therefore think no more of it and do not less us pass remarks on onnecessary subjects. Biddy give herself a deal of trouble with me afore I left (for I am awful dull) as I should view it in this light, and viewing it in this light, I find it so.

    Pause.

And now you are better, Pip?

Pip Yes, Joe. Thank you.

Joe Then I shall be on my way home.

Pip But Joe!

Joe Like I said to you, Pip, divisions amongst men must come. I am not fit for your company here, you a gentleman and with money and expectations, and so I take my leave.

    Joe fetches his coat.

Pip But Joe. I am not a gentleman. I have no money! Joe!

    Exit Joe. Pip pauses, then writes a letter on his writing desk.

Dear Biddy, I present this letter myself to you today, humbled and repentant. I must tell you how I have lost all

I had once hoped for. Biddy, I think you once liked me well, when my heart was quieter and better than it ever has been since. If you can like me half as well once more, if you can take me with all my faults and disappointments on my head, if you can receive me like a forgiven child, and, dear Biddy, if you can tell me that you will go through the world with me, you will surely make it a better world for me, and me a better man for it, and I will try hard to make it a better world for you.

Pip seals the letter and puts it in his pocket, before leaving his rooms.

The forge. Biddy and Joe are greeting Pip, who has just arrived. They are in fine clothes. Pip stands before them, having just arrived, in shock. He has half-taken the letter out of his pocket.

Pip Biddy?

Biddy Hello, dear Pip!

Pip But dear Biddy, how smart you are!

Biddy Yes, dear Pip.

Pip And Joe, how smart you are!

Joe Yes, dear Pip, old chap.

Pause. Joe slowly places his hand around Biddy's waist.

You see, old chap . . .

Biddy It's my wedding day. And I am married to Joe!

FIFTEEN

Eleven years later. Joe is sitting by the old fire smoking in his smithy clothes. The scene is exactly reminiscent of the second scene, and indeed there is a small boy sitting where Pip sat, writing on a blackboard. But the boy is the puppet-boy from the first scene. Pip knocks at the door to the forge and enters.

Joe Pip. Dear Pip! How long?

Pip Eleven years, Joe.

Joe How was your travels? The East?

Pip The East was well, Joe. And this is . . .

Joe We give him the name of Pip, for your sake, dear chap. And we hoped he might grow a little like him and we think he do.

Pip bends down and kisses the boy gently on the cheeks.

Pip I think so too. May I take him for a walk tomorrow?

Joe By all means, Pip. Where will you take him?

The graveyard. The sound of the sea rises on the wind as they sit in silence. Pip takes the puppet-boy and perches him on the tombstone of Phillip Pirrip and also Georgiana.

Pip 'Here lies Philip Pirrip, late of this parish, and also Georgiana, wife of the above.'
    Let me set you up upon the stone.

Pip helps the puppet-boy clamber up on the tombstone.
Pip turns away to stare at the sea. The puppet-boy
takes out the crust of bread and eats. Pip stares at
him.
    A shadow rises from behind the grave . . .
    It is Estella. Older. Quite altered, in a full coat.
Signs of a cruel life upon her face.

Estella I heard you had returned.

Pip Estella?

Estella I am greatly changed. I wonder you know me.

Pip Do you often come back?

Estella I have never come since.

Pip Nor I.

Estella Satis House is to be built on. I came up to take leave of it before its change. And you? You live abroad still?

Pip Still.

Estella And do well, I am sure.

Pip I work pretty hard for a living, and therefore – yes, I do well. (*Pause.*) I was told that you separated from your husband. That he used you with great cruelty.

    Pause.

Estella I have often thought of you.

Pip Have you?

Estella Of late very often.

Pip You have always held a place in my heart.

    Pause.

Estella I little thought that, in taking leave of the house, I should be taking leave of you. I am very glad to do so.

Pip Glad to part again, Estella? To me parting is a painful thing. Remembrance of our last parting has been ever mournful and painful.

Estella But you said to me, 'God bless you, God forgive you!' And if you could say that to me then, you will not hesitate to say that to me now – now, when suffering has been stronger than all other teaching, and has taught me to understand what your heart used to be. I have been bent and broken but – I hope – into a better shape. Be as considerate and as good to me as you were, and tell me we are friends.

Pip We are friends.

Estella And will continue friends apart.

She holds out her hand to him and he takes it and kisses it. She does not let go. Long silence, apart from the sea and the gentle chewing of the puppet-boy. He looks at the couple as he sits eating his bread . . .

The End.